GOING,
GOING, GONE...

GOING, GOING, GONE...

The History, Lore, and Mystique of the Home Run

Major League Baseball Properties
Robert Creamer
Elias Sports Bureau
David Halberstam
Donald Honig
Leonard Koppett

Ed Linn
Ray Robinson
Lee Schreiber
Berry Stainback
Bobby Thomson

Edited by BRIAN SILVERMAN

HarperResource
An Imprint of HarperCollinsPublishers

HarperCollins books may be purchased for educational, business, or sales promotional use. For information, please write to: Special Markets Department, HarperCollins Publishers Inc., 10 East 53rd Street, New York, New York 10022.

FIRST EDITION

Designed by Jerry Wilke

Printed on acid-free paper

Library of Congress Cataloging-in-Publication Data

     Going, going, gone...: the history, lore and mystique of the home run / Major League Baseball Properties ; [written by] Bobby Thomson... [et al.]; edited by Brian Silverman. 1st ed.
        p. cm
        ISBN 0-06-105165-9
        1. Home runs (Baseball) 2. Baseball–United States–History.
        3. Baseball players–United States. I. Thomson, Bobby, 1923–II. Silverman, Brian. III. Major League Baseball Properties, Inc.

     GV868.4 .G65 2000
     796.357'0973–dc21
                                  99-059437

00 01 02 03 04 RRD 10 9 8 7 6 5 4 3 2 1

Dedicated to baseball fans everywhere.

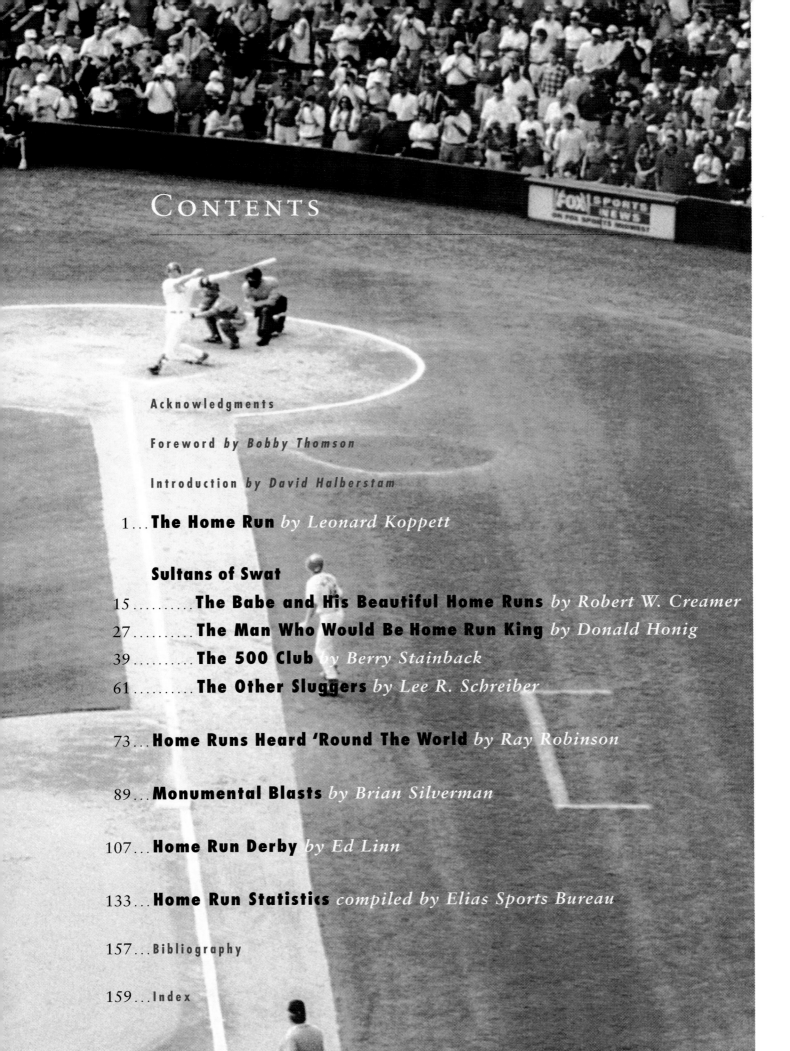

CONTENTS

ACKNOWLEDGMENTS

John Silbersack was the first to take an interest in the idea, and his kick-start made it a go. Robert Wilson was also there at the beginning, and his vision was essential to the project. Don Hintze at Major League Baseball was an enthusiastic supporter of the project and helped guide it smoothly to completion. Charlie Butler and Charles Salzberg provided their estimable editorial skills. Mike McCormack at Major League Baseball, and Steve Hirdt of the Elias Sports Bureau were both amazingly quick to respond to my sometimes desperate and vague pleas for help. The accurate eye of Walter Friedman was essential for poring over the manuscript for any misinformation, factual or numerical. I doubt there is anyone who knows more about the home run than David Vincent, and he was gracious in sharing his vast knowledge with me. Finding photographs was, at times, daunting, but made much easier with the help of Paul Cunningham and Rich Pilling at Major League Baseball, and Tom Gilbert at AP/Wide World Photos. I would also like to thank the Society of American Baseball Research (SABR). Others who made contributions with their help, knowledge, insights, support, and observations include Kristin Hillen, Roger Angell, and the members of Ernie's Round Table: Marty Appel, Larry Ritter, David Falkner, Stan Isaacs, and Lee Lowenfish. Finally, none of this would have been possible without the love and support of Heather Jackson and the wisdom and guidance of Al Silverman.

*Though Henry Louis Aaron and Louis Gehrig were never factors
in the naming of the newest addition to my life,
Louis Anthony Silverman, to whom this book is dedicated,
it bodes well that he too may one day experience
what it feels like to hit a home run.*
B. S.

FOREWORD

by Bobby Thomson

Bobby Thomson (center right) and Leo Durocher rejoice in the locker room after the game-winning home run.

EDITOR'S NOTE: *Bobby Thomson was a three-time National League All-Star, batted in 100 runs or more in four different seasons, and hit 264 home runs in an impressive fifteen-year Major League career. Yet he is generally remembered for one home run—The Shot Heard 'Round the World. Considered to be the most dramatic home run in baseball history, Thomson's heroic ninth-inning, three-run home run to win the National League pennant for the New York Giants on October 3, 1951 has been the subject of countless articles, books, and documentaries. In May 1998, the U.S. Postal Service issued a postage stamp commemorating the event. Here, Thomson discusses what a home run means to him and recalls some of the details of his mythic home run.*

Home runs for the most part represent the biggest thrill in baseball. It's what attracts fans to the ballpark. Witness the attention paid to the Mark McGwire–Sammy Sosa home run race of 1998 and again last season. Baseball fans, young and old, were caught up in the thrill and excitement of the home run.

The thing that sticks in my mind about home runs is that they win ball games. They can turn defeat into victory. I was fortunate enough to have had the opportunity to hit a game-winning home run for the Giants that came to be called The Shot Heard 'Round the World.

What was amounting in 1951 to a lost season—we were thirteen and a half games behind the Brooklyn Dodgers on August 11th—turned out to be a tie by season's end, forcing a three-game playoff to decide the National League pennant. Two home runs—one by me and one by Monte Irvin—won the first game for the Giants. Great pitching by Brooklyn shut down our hitting in the second game for a Dodgers victory. The third and deciding game set the stage for the "almighty" home run.

A feeling of depression followed us into the last of the ninth inning, losing by a score of 4–1, with Dodger pitcher Don Newcombe having shut us down in the eighth inning by striking out the side. Entering the dugout, I slammed my glove to the ground, realizing as the fifth batter in the inning that I might not even get a chance to hit.

But before I knew it, Alvin Dark hit a ground ball through the infield for a single and Don Mueller followed with another grounder through the infield for a base hit, putting runners on first and third with no outs. Monte Irvin, without whom we wouldn't have reached this point in the season, popped up for the first out. Then Whitey Lockman doubled to left, making the score 4 to 2, with runners on second and third.

It was at this point, in my mind, that the whole situation changed.

Sliding into third base, Mueller severely injured his ankle. As the next batter, I hustled to Mueller, lying on the ground in real pain. In retrospect, this incident took my mind completely off the game. It wasn't until Mueller was carried off the field that my mind actually returned to the game at hand.

People have asked me what it was like walking up the third base line to home plate, and what the crowd was like. I can honestly say that I was in my own little world at the time—in a mindset I had never before been in during a ball game.

Walking to home plate I began to psyche myself up, telling myself to do a good job, wait and watch for the ball, don't get overanxious. I was getting back to the fundamentals of hitting. I was also calling myself an S.O.B. to make myself more determined and more aggressive. It wasn't until I reached home plate that I realized the Dodgers had changed pitchers.

Waiting and watching, I took the first pitch down the middle of the plate for a strike. The guys on the bench told me later they wanted to kill me for taking that first pitch. The next pitch was a fastball inside and high, and I remember just getting a glimpse of it. I had been hitting pretty well for the last three months and the quickness of my hands and the groove I was in allowed me to get around on it and pull it to left field.

I made good contact and my first thought was *home run, upper deck*. Then I watched the ball begin to sink—apparently I had gotten slightly on top of it. My next thought was *it's just a base hit*. The next thing I knew the ball disappeared into the lower stands and suddenly I felt an emotion I had never experienced before. I hyperventilated as I ran around the base paths, jumped onto home plate and into the arms of my teammates.

Much has been said and written about the home run. I think that's for a number of reasons. For starters, the Giants had overcome a thirteen and a half game deficit. Then we overcame a three-run lead in the bottom of the ninth inning in the final game of the season. Further burning the memory into people's minds was the now-famous call by broadcaster Russ Hodges (*"The Giants win the pennant, the Giants win the pennant . . ."*), not to mention the fierce rivalry between the Dodgers and Giants, and the glare of the New York press.

Over the years, I have enjoyed meeting people who have approached me, anxious to tell me their story of where they were and what they were doing at the time of the home run. It's amazing how much of an impact one swing of the bat can make on so many lives. Especially if that swing just happens to be a game-winning home run. Not everyone remembers the single, or the stolen base, but everyone seems to remember the home run. It's the most exciting event in baseball. To be part of a book that celebrates that event is an honor and a thrill.

INTRODUCTION

by David Halberstam

This happened a long time ago in another century, on August 10, 1946 to be exact, but the memory is as clear as if it happened yesterday—clearer, to tell the truth, because yesterday's deeds seem to vanish with approaching old age ever more quickly into the fog of mundane daily rituals. The occasion was my brother's fourteenth birthday and we were living, as we had during the war, in Winsted, Connecticut. My father had returned from serving overseas after more than three years away, and he had bought tickets for that day's Yankees–Red Sox game. They were box seats, purchased eagerly much earlier in the season in the hope of a tight pennant race. Box seats, in a family such as ours, represented a considerable financial splurge. But it was the Yankees playing the Red Sox, a historic rivalry amplified by regional tensions, and in that particular period, by the Williams–DiMaggio competition and the endless debate as to which one of these icons was the better player.

In 1946 the Red Sox, bolstered by what was for them an unusually strong pitching staff, had taken a huge lead on their would-be pursuers. Their star players, Ted Williams, Bobby Doerr, and Dom DiMaggio, had adjusted readily to the game after the long wartime absences, while the Yankee players, most notably Joe DiMaggio, had struggled to get their timing back. The Sox would eventually win the pennant by 12 games over Detroit, with the Yankees a bad third, 17 games back.

That the game was no longer important in terms of a would-be pennant race mattered little to my brother or me—I was all of twelve. It was a big league baseball game, the Yankees and the Red Sox, and for the first time a game that I would truly be able to comprehend; the last game I had seen had been five years earlier, before the war, and my understanding of the game and its intricacies was far more marginal then. In the ensuing years I had remained not so much faithful as *addicted* to the sport, guided by Mel Allen ("That ball is going, going . . . it is *gone!*") and Red Barber and their talk about Ballantine Blasts, White Owl Wallops, and Old Goldies. In our house in Winsted, a hundred miles from New York where the signal from WINS 1010 was often frail, we had learned which parts of the house and which angles to hold the radio delivered the clearest reception.

This trip then was an ultimate kind of reward, in effect a postwar present for the Allies defeating the Axis, a pleasure long deferred. In these days when so many games are on so many different television channels every weekend, it is hard to imagine how important a chance to go to the Stadium or to Fenway actually was in those pre-sport-glut days.

On that day, famous at least in my mind, the Yankees won 7–5 in extra innings. And it was a home run that did it. Aaron Robinson, a journeyman Yankee catcher, hit his second home run of the day in the twelfth inning to win it. Ted Williams also hit two home runs that day. And what I remember most clearly, one of my handful of sacred memories, was that one of Williams's home runs was a vicious shot off Tiny Bonham. I think of it as the hardest hit ball I have ever seen— whether it is or not, I have no idea, but the important thing is that I think it was, and therefore it stands clear and unchallenged in my own memory bank.

Williams hit, with the full force of his classic swing, a savage line drive that rose majestically. And it kept rising and rising, landing well into the third tier. In another time, one more given to the marking of special achievements might have painted the seat where the ball landed. But the only memorial to it is the one that remains in my memory. And in my memory there was an audible gasp on the part of the immense crowd, followed by a hushed silence because it was a predominantly Yankee crowd.

The film clips of that general era tend to portray Williams before his body thickened, still willowy and gangly, a boy hitting like a man, but I have no memory of which Williams it was who swung that day, the skinny kid or the heftier Williams of later memory. I like to think I can remember Williams circling the bases. He had a very private home run trot, head down, as if the moment belonged solely to him and not to the fans, but clearly he took a quiet special pleasure of hitting well in New York in Yankee Stadium, in DiMaggio's house, as it were. But it may be that this is the work of my imagination aided by countless film clips on Classic Sports Network, and that I have come to remember now what I did not remember three or four years after the event.

Some forty-two years later when I got to know Williams and we became, in a kind of tentative way, pals, I mentioned that moment which had first joined us, and as I told the story I saw the smile slowly begin to spread over his face. I had, knowing what I knew about him by then, come to believe that he remembered every pitch thrown to him at every at-bat by every pitcher—pitchers being, by his own description, dumb by breed. I was sure he remembered everything about the moment: the day, the particular lighting in the Stadium, what Tiny Bonham had thrown on the previous pitch, and therefore what Bonham was going to throw on this pitch, how right his calculation had been, and, of course, the awesome trajectory of the ball. We were on this day of remembrance in 1988 somewhat short of other witnesses to the moment—Tiny Bonham died in 1949, and my brother and father had died before I finally met Williams—but I remembered thinking as we spoke and as I saw that knowing smile: *Ted Williams remembers, too; he remembers Tiny Bonham, and the pitch and where it finally landed.*

I am fascinated to this day at why that memory is so clear when so many others of seemingly greater import to my life have long since faded. I have covered wars and revolutions, and written sixteen books in the interim. And that game was a long time ago, not even midpoint in a century already gone: To measure how distant a moment it was, remember that it took place nine days before the current President of the United States, William Jefferson Clinton, was born. It is, I think, just one more example of the baseball fan's love of the home run, which I suspect is part of the American fan's addiction not just to sport, but to explosions of power—to the slam-dunk in basketball, the long touchdown pass or bomb in football, and the knockout punch in boxing. In baseball the equation is simple: one swing and we often get a new ballgame.

In the ensuing years I have thrilled again and again to great home runs, particularly those that bring with them a certain sudden death quality, the home runs, as it were, of finality, completely altering a given outcome. All of these I have either seen—sometimes electronically—or heard: Bobby Thomson off Ralph Branca, Bill Mazerowski off Ralph Terry, Kirk Gibson off Dennis Eckersley, Carlton Fisk off Pat Darcy.

I am left with images of other perhaps less dramatic moments: of Mantle and Maris in that marvelous 1961 assault upon the Ruth record; Mantle oversized in everything, with that massive swing (Pedro Ramos once told me of one stunning tape measure home run that Mantle had hit off him in the Stadium, that when he last saw it, the ball looked like it was on its way to Connecticut); Maris always knowing his limitations, probably sure that the whole chase was a perverse joke played upon him by the gods—placing him in New York in the first place, competing against a friend for a record he did not really want (certainly not at the expense of his treasured anonymity) but playing almost perfectly that season with his measured, compact swing. Hank Aaron, Bad Henry the pitchers called him, somehow looked less like a home run hitter than most of the others but with those magnificent wrists was able to hit the ball at the very last nanosecond. Willie Mays, though exciting in every aspect of the game, was sentenced to play so much of his career in windblown Candlestick Park. (When he had first walked around it, he had turned to a friend with a certain dismay, knowing what its odd, windy location might mean to his career and his home run totals, and asked, "Why don't they ever consult the ballplayers when they build a new park?")

In recent years I have thrilled again to the race between Mark McGwire and Sammy Sosa, a race that was so much fun to watch because they were both so good, and because they both behaved with singular charm and elegance, and because they seemed to represent ethnically both the old America and the new, and yet they liked and admired each other and made it fun for the fans. McGwire is, to me, a surprisingly supple hitter for such a big man, able, as few men of his sheer size are, to make instantaneous adjustments with his hands against truly gifted pitchers. Sosa is immensely powerful, big in the chest and shoulders, a quick reminder of how much more powerful athletes are today than they were forty years ago.

I should note here, I love well-pitched ball games. Offered a choice between an 8–6 game or a 2–1 game, I will always take the latter. I love the idea of two excellent pitchers going at it—if at all possible for the full nine innings—with the capacity of one batter in the late innings to change the entire game with just one swing. The late innings are filled with pure drama, power pitcher daring power hitter, power hitter daring power pitcher.

I have often pondered why Americans seem to love home runs, why the McGwire–Sosa race seemed to create even more excitement than the pennant race itself that year. I think one reason is that time matters in this country, more in this century and the latter half of the old one than in the past. As a people we are always in a hurry, we dare not rest on our laurels, jobs and positions in life are rarely passed on from father to son and from mother to daughter, and we do not have time, even in our time off, for slow-motion, languid recreation. We want drama and instant gratification and the home run often provides that.

Babe Ruth changed the nature of the game, thereby meeting the needs of a changing America, one that was going from rural to urban, from slow-paced society to an ever faster pace. Starting in 1920 when as a Yankee Ruth had his first full season as a regular and hit 54 home runs—more than any other team in baseball except the Phillies—he not only gave the game a bigger bang for a buck, he offered drama every time he came to bat. We are all, I think, in the Babe's debt, for he changed and modernized the game, and made it more exciting and brought the element of power to it.

And so I think of what I have seen in the previous century: DiMaggio, with his bat cocked at a seemingly exaggerated angle, legs spread wide, a great classic swing; Williams, always so graceful, as if he were born to do one thing: swing a baseball bat from the left side; Mays and Aaron and Frank Robinson; Maris and Mantle in their wonderful race against one of the great records in the book; Reggie Jackson in that one magical World Series game when he nailed three; Kirk Gibson limping to the plate to change the outcome; and Carlton Fisk using body language to keep his game winner fair. And then, at the end of the century, the majestic home run battles of McGwire and Sosa, the steady, consistent power of Junior Griffey, and an unlikely hero named Chad Curtis, in the last World Series of the century, pumping his arms in the air after delivering the winning blow, reminding us that, as it was when the Babe was thrilling the crowds in the 1920s, it is still the home run that, in baseball, moves us like nothing else.

Chad Curtis (center top) celebrates with his Yankee teammates after smashing a 10th inning home run to win game 3 of the last World Series of the twentieth century.

score any point. Others must block or clear out an area for the actual scorer in football, basketball, hockey, or soccer. Even the apparent exception, basketball's free throw, results only if someone commits a foul.

But the home run hitter stands up there all by himself, receiving a legal pitch, just like the hundred or more being delivered to all batters, and only when it is his designated turn in the batting order. He can hit the ball into fair territory only once during that time at bat, and can score "his own" run only by hitting the ball out of every defender's reach. If other base runners precede him, so much the better, but his own score is accomplished without anyone else's help.

Spectators caught on to this special quality of the "home run hit" right from the start. "To hit a home run" passed into everyday language as a metaphor for maximum success in any enterprise—individual success for team benefit, without the aid of teammates. Other sports do not provide the same image. A touchdown, a field goal, a basket, a hockey or soccer goal can't be disconnected from teammate activity, whoever gets credit for the actual points. But when we say someone—or something—"hits a home run," sole responsibility for that glory is unambiguous.

In baseball's early years, most home runs were drives that went between and beyond the outfielders, giving the batter enough time to race around the bases before the ball could be retrieved and thrown homeward.

Even when games began to be played in enclosed grounds, the mushy ball seldom reached a distant barrier on the fly. But when professionalism took hold and "baseball grounds" were built specifically for that purpose, a drive that flew (or bounced) over an outfield fence became an automatic home run and a triumphant jog around the bases.

Either way, that's what spectators wanted to see. And remember. And talk about. And compare to other such blows. And to honor the remarkable player who could do that more often than the rest.

And it didn't take long for the professional promoters to recognize a good thing—and overdo it.

When Major League play began, in the 1870s, home runs were rare. The ball was relatively dead, and kept in play as long as possible while being battered and scuffed, and pitchers had learned many ways to fool hitters. It was not good form, nor good tactics, for most players to try to hit for distance, since the longer a fly ball stayed in the air, the more time a fielder had to catch up with it. The right way to hit was to use a level swing to produce line drives or hard grounders that shot through the infield, or soft liners purposely placed over infielders' heads.

But the *possibility* of a home run, in any time at bat, caused a constant undercurrent of excitement among the fans, aware how dramatically it might affect winning or losing the game. If a home run was such a good thing, wouldn't more home runs be a better thing?

> *"It might be! It could be! It is! Holy cow!"*
> —**HARRY CARAY**, Hall of Fame broadcaster

In the 1880s, the Chicago White Stockings had emerged as the first dominant team of the National League's first decade. They won pennants in 1880, 1881, and 1882. Their celebrity made money for others when they brought their glamor to other cities, and for themselves at home. But in 1883, when they moved into a new ballpark (on the site of the old one, which had burned down), they were beaten out by Boston.

Their new home field—called Lake Front Park II by ballpark historians—had the smallest playing area ever used.

Its right-field foul line was only 186 feet, to a six-foot-high fence. Center field was no more than 300 feet deep. Left field was only 190 feet, but topped by a 37-foot wood-and-canvas wall. The right-field fence was so low and close to home that balls hit over it became automatic doubles, according to ground rules that a home team had the right to make. (Some sources say that left field was the short one, but contemporary illustrations show it to be right field.)

Such dimensions lessened the advantage Chicago enjoyed by having three outstanding pitchers, instead of the then-customary two, and Boston's more powerful hitting team won the championship. Until 1883, no team had hit more than 20 homers in a season, and no player as many as 10. That year, with the schedule increased from 84 to 98 games, Boston hit 34 while New York's Buck Ewing hit 10 of his team's 24. In the new but less respected American Association, Harry Stovey hit 14.

Chicago hit only 13—and 277 doubles.

The White Stocking brain trust—Albert Spalding, club president, and Cap Anson, star player and manager—decided to change the ground rules. Now anything hit over the right-field fence would be a home run, not merely a double. Chicago hitters would have the benefit of that in all their 56 home games (in a schedule expanded to 112); a visitor like Boston would get only eight such chances.

So the White Stockings hit 142 homers in 1884, while no other club hit more than 39 (Buffalo). Ned Williamson hit 27, Fred Pfeffer 25, Abner Dalrymple 22, and Anson 21. Buffalo's Dan Brouthers was

4

In 1884 A.G. Spalding (opposite bottom) and Cap Anson (left) changed the ground rules in Chicago, awarding balls hit over the right-field fence to be home runs, not doubles, as was previously ruled.

fifth in the league with 14. Chicago's total of doubles was 162, so the net result of 115 fewer doubles and 129 more homers was due entirely to the new ground rules. Of Chicago's 142 homers, 131 were hit at home. Those four 20-homer men, who had hit a total of four in the same park in 1883 (and two on the road), hit 88 at home and only 7 away in 1884.

Nevertheless, it didn't work out the way Spalding and Anson had hoped. Their pitchers gave up 83 homers, 66 of them at home, and the club finished tied for fourth place.

Yes, it was possible to gimmick up too much of a good thing.

The next year, the White Stockings, now called "Anson's Colts," moved into a new home, West Side Park, which had an oval shape (like New York's later Polo Grounds) with a bicycle track circling the field. The foul lines were short (216 feet to a 12-foot wall) but the rest of the outfield was spacious and pitchers had a chance to avoid the short homers.

Back to playing real baseball, Chicago proceeded to win the pennant in 1885 and 1886, giving it five championships in seven years. Williamson's home run total in 1885 fell from 27 to 3, Pfeffer's from 25 to 5, Anson's from 21 to 7—while Dalrymple's 11 led the league.

In the fourteen seasons after 1884, only once did a player reach 20 homers: Philadelphia's Sam Thompson in a 138-game schedule in 1889. When Washington's Buck Freeman hit 25 in a 154-game schedule ten years later, the 1899 season was such a disaster that he got little attention. A twelve-team Major League monopoly since 1892, the National League dropped four of its teams (including Washington) for the 1900 season. The American League didn't claim major status until 1901. Baseball interest was at a low point.

So Williamson's artificial record of 27 remained indelibly in the books—and widely ignored—until Ruth broke it in 1919.

In the intervening years, the number 20 had

Benefiting from the rule change of Spalding and Anson was Ned Williamson (below) of the White Sox, who hit 27 homers in 1884.

5

been reached twice. In 1911, when a livelier ball was introduced, Frank Schulte of Chicago (now called the Cubs) led the National League with 21. And in 1915, Gavvy Cravath of the Phillies, the true pre-Ruth home run king, hit 24 with a re-deadened ball. Cravath led the league in homers six times in seven years (1912–19), twice with 19, and once (1918) with as few as 8.

But no American Leaguer had ever reached 20 when Ruth, Boston's star left-handed pitcher, started playing the outfield frequently in 1918.

He had joined the Red Sox in 1914, and helped them become World Series winners in 1915 and 1916. In 1917, he won 24 and lost 13 with six shutouts and a 2.01 earned-run average, completing 35 of 38 starts as the Red Sox finished second to Chicago.

In 1918, a season abruptly shortened by World War I, the Red Sox won another World Series. Ed Barrow had become Boston's manager, and did what Ruth's teammates and fans had been wondering about. He let him play the outfield in 59 games so that he could bat, and started him as a pitcher only 19 times. His pitching record was 13–7, and in 317 at-bats, Ruth tied for the league lead with 11 homers—all on the road. Fenway Park's contours, then as now, did not favor a left-handed slugger.

So in 1919, in a 140-game season, Ruth made only 15 starts (going 9–5) and played 115 in the field—and hit 29 home runs, 20 of them on the road. Williamson's record, its phony aspects long forgotten, had finally been surpassed.

The reaction was astonishment. The 1920 *Spalding Baseball Guide*, the sport's most authoritative editorial voice, marveled that on August 23–25 Ruth had hit four home runs in three days, a "whirlwind of batting."

"Perhaps, and very likely, Ruth will

6

In 1918 the Boston Red Sox star left-handed pitcher, Babe Ruth, started 59 games in the outfield and tied for the league lead in homers with 11.

HOME RUN TERMINOLOGY

Tater. Dinger. Longball. Roundtripper. Four-bagger.
Circuit clout. Shot. Bomb. Knock. Big knock. Big fly.
Big salami (grand slam). Going deep. Going yard.
Parking it. Dial 8. Jake. Touch 'em all.
Elvis has left the building.

not be so successful in 1920," wrote John B. Foster, the *Guide*'s editor. "The pitchers will eye him with more than ordinary caution."

So in 1920, he hit 54. And then 59 in 1921. And all baseball was changed forever.

It was not an accident. After the 1919 season, the club owners installed some basic changes. They restored the schedule to 154 games, realizing they had played too few in 1919. They noted the excitement caused by Ruthian high-arc, long-distance blasts, and remembered that when they had tried a livelier baseball in 1911 and 1912, there had been a marked uptick in attendance. The idea that the public liked homers and high scoring had finally sunk in. So they made the ball substantially more lively and, more to the point, instructed the umpires to keep a fresh ball in play as much as possible. At the same time, they outlawed all sorts of trick pitches—notably the spitball—but also other ways of scuffing or discoloring the ball, giving batters a better look at less difficult deliveries of a ball that would go further when hit squarely.

If one Babe Ruth was such an attraction, why not others?

Then, in January, the Red Sox sold Ruth to the New York Yankees.

Now his prodigious clouts would have center stage in every respect. The Yankees were tenants of the Giants in the Polo Grounds, the oldest park with the largest seating capacity in the nation's biggest city.

No one imagined he'd hit 54. No other whole team in the American League hit more than 50. No other player hit more than George Sisler's 19. Then, just as the 1920 season was ending, the news broke that the 1919 World Series had been fixed. Ruth's extraordinary feats became the only available positive conversational material to counterbalance the negativism of the whole awful Chicago Black Sox story.

But, welcome as it was, that was a transient benefit.

What really mattered was that Ruth showed other players, and all managers, how long-ball hitting could dominate and win ball games. All the best hitters were still level-swing practitioners. Ruth had an uppercut stroke which, once seen, could be mastered by others.

In 1921, two runners-up hit 24, two others 23, and one 21.

In 1922, when illness limited Ruth to 35, Rogers Hornsby hit 42, Ken Williams 39, and Tilly Walker 37.

In 1923, Ruth and Cy Williams hit 41 each, and Ken Williams 29.

By 1925 there were eleven players hitting 20 or more.

In 1927, when Ruth hit 60, Gehrig had 47, Hack Wilson 30, Cy Williams 30.

During the 1950s, hitting 20 was done an average of twenty-nine times a year, still with 16 teams playing 154 games. In 1999 alone, in a 162-game season, and with 30 teams, it was done 103 times. Before 1920, teams averaged less than one homer every six games; by the middle 1920s, one in every three; from 1934 on, more than one in every two; since 1993, more than one a game.

Home run frequency has been a steadily rising graph while batting averages have been slowly declining.

This is the revolution Ruth wrought. Those capable of hitting lots of homers learn (and are taught) to swing for them, with an uppercut stroke. Most players don't have that special ability, and should be level-swing hitters—but almost all succumb to the long-ball temptation sometimes. The price is more strikeouts and lower averages, but the trade-off seems worth it from the team point of view. After all, the home run does change the score 100 percent of the time, no matter

8

In 1922 Rogers Hornsby (above) of the St. Louis Cardinals led the National League in homers with 42.

who hits it when. Singles and doubles may, but they may not. No one is left on base when a homer is hit.

> *"Get upstairs, Aunt Minnie, and raise the window!"*
> —**ALBERT KENNEDY "ROSEY" ROSWELL**, Pittsburgh Pirates radio announcer

This, in turn, has revolutionized pitching. Getting a batter to hit a fly ball used to be considered desirable for the pitcher, most likely to produce an out, so "high strikes" were "good" pitches. But if a substantial number of those flies might hit or clear a fence, you had better avoid them. Now you want grounders, most of which infielders can handle—especially if the batter is trying to hit a long ball. So "pitch low" is the order of the day, since even the weaker hitters may hit one out if you get the ball "up."

Striking out used to be considered a sin and an embarrassment: It's a totally unproductive out that can't advance any runner or give a fielder a chance to make an error. Ruth's 1,330 strikeouts were a record when he retired, but his appeal was such that fans oohed and aahed at his swing even when he missed. But he never struck out 100 times in one season; by now, a player has fanned at least 146 times in one year 110 times.

Today, there is no sense of shame attached to a strikeout. Most players (but not managers!) feel the occasional home run—which they wouldn't get if they didn't swing hard—justifies the unproductive out.

Baserunning is affected. You don't risk a failed steal or hit-and-run as often if the man at bat has a reasonable chance of getting a homer or extra-base hit. It all depends, of course, on who's at bat and who's pitching how (which is true of everything in baseball all the time). But the free-swinging approach, derided as "unscientific" and "unskilled" before Ruth, is now the universally accepted style of play.

Hack Wilson (below) hit 30 home runs in 1927 to tie for the National League lead with Cy Williams. Despite leading the league, Wilson and Williams were 17 and 30 home runs, respectively, behind the American League leaders Lou Gehrig and Babe Ruth in that memorable home run–hitting season.

9

10

The House That Ruth Built...Yankee Stadium.

Hank Aaron impressed on Dusty Baker, the San Francisco Giants manager and one of his disciples, the importance of weighing correctly the risk versus benefit factor in any baseball decision. Ruth changed those equations for all time. Once the benefit of a home run became realistically attainable instead of an occasional accident, every other aspect of baseball risk assessment changed, too.

*"I am the king of the diamond.
Let there be an abundant clubhouse feast!
Bring me the finest meats and cheeses in the land."*
—**KENNY MAYNE,** ESPN

As for the fans, they love homers and always have. Baseball's most famous poem, "Casey at the Bat," written in the 1880s, has as its premise that Mudville expects its hero Casey, with two on and two out and his team two runs behind in the bottom of the ninth, to hit a game-winning homer.

That graph showing the steady increase in home run frequency is paralleled by the graph of rising attendance. Many other factors are involved, it goes without saying, but the fact remains that more runs sell more tickets—and more home runs produce more runs.

The relationship between attendance and home runs is even more direct. Originally, in the nineteenth century (and in the minor leagues always), grandstands were concentrated around the infield area and seldom went as far as the ends of the foul lines. The outfield fences usually marked the outer boundary of the property, so at least in some direction (usually center) they were very far from home plate.

As crowds increased, additional seats were added, as outfield bleachers or extensions of the grandstand to the foul line. Since the contour of the property didn't change, the added sections were within the field of play in the outfield, bringing playing-field fences in. The over-the-fence homer became not only more frequent and more attainable, but automatic. The inside-the-park homer depended on fast running, and the strongest hitters were not always the fastest. So the risk-benefit equation changed as the playing surface shrank.

Brooklyn's fabled Ebbets Field was a good example of this process. When built in 1913, the double-decked grandstand ended just beyond third base and at the right field corner, seating 18,000. The left field fence (against the street) was 419 feet at the foul line, 450 or more in center. Right field, hemmed in by the other side of the square block being occupied, was always short (300 to 350 feet) but with a high concrete fence, eventually made even higher with a screen.

By 1926, open bleachers were installed in left field, making that foul line 384 feet (and capacity 28,000).

In 1931, the double-decked grandstand was extended around left field as far as center. Now the left-field foul line was about 350 feet, with center still 440, soon cut to 400. Then box seats were added to the front of the left-field stands, so when the Boys of Summer in the 1950s had their legendary seasons, it was 343 feet down the left-field line and only 383 to center, with the barrier itself lower than it used to be.

Similar "filling in" took place at many of the parks built between 1910 and 1915, which became baseball's stabilized venue until the 1960s. As outfields shrank, home runs increased. Wrigley Field and Fenway Park, the two most hallowed "old" parks still in use, had much larger center fields originally. Yankee Stadium, rebuilt in 1975, is now 399 feet in left center where it was once 490, and 385 in right center where it was once 429, and 408 in straight center field where it was once 490.

BALLPARKS WITH THE MOST HOMERS THROUGH 1999

1. Tiger Stadium...10,878
2. Wrigley Field...9,836
3. Yankee Stadium...9,372
4. Fenway Park...9,255
5. Sportsman's Park III...8,268
6. Shibe Park...6,965
7. Cleveland Stadium...6,659
8. Polo Grounds V...6,657
9. Comiskey Park I...6,250
10. County Stadium...5,490

Fenway Park and the famed "Green Monster" looming in left field (right).

12

Tiger Stadium (left), where more home runs were hit than anywhere else, closed its doors after the 1999 season.

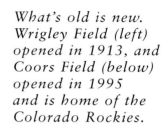

What's old is new. Wrigley Field (left) opened in 1913, and Coors Field (below) opened in 1995 and is home of the Colorado Rockies.

13

The wonderful new parks in Baltimore, Cleveland, Denver, Texas, and a half dozen others in the works try to re-create the atmosphere and irregular layouts of the 1910-15 parks, and all are as homer-friendly as those had become by the 1950s.

Bill Veeck, that most astute of baseball promoters, taught that it's not enough to produce an exciting event in front of comfortable customers. "It must," he declared, "cause conversation."

Nothing causes as much baseball talk as home runs. They are baseball's most distinctive and most essential feature. Long may they fly.

"Going . . . Going . . . Gone!"
—**MEL ALLEN,** New York Yankee broadcaster

The Babe and His Beautiful Home Runs

Robert W. Creamer

One big reason why Babe Ruth's name is so inextricably linked with the home run is the huge impact he made on the art of hitting a ball over a fence after he burst onto the baseball scene in 1914. Before the Babe came along, homers were nothing much. Triples, for example, were hit far more often, and because inside-the-park homers were relatively common back then, the home run for the most part was looked upon as a stretch-limo triple, much the way today's triple is looked upon as an extended double. Homers were a minor part of the game. Evidence? Batting statistics printed in newspapers in the first decades of the twentieth century listed league leaders in such areas as stolen bases and sacrifice bunts, but not home runs.

Sure, home runs were hit and, sure, they were admired. Frank "Home Run" Baker showed how glamorous the homer could be when he whacked a couple of dramatic blasts in the 1911 World Series to earn his indelible nickname.

Even earlier, back in the 1880s and 1890s, there had been a rash of home runs, but that upsurge in long-distance slugging had early baseball purists moaning that home runs were ruining the game.

By the early 1900s the tide had ebbed; when Ruth was a kid growing up in St. Mary's School in Baltimore, Major League home run championships were won with as few as 9, 8, even 7 in a season. Few of those were McGwire-type boomers. Most were inside-the-park jobs or long flies that barely cleared not-too-distant outfield fences.

Then Ruth appeared. Later in his career it was the extraordinary number of homers that he hit and the drama of the moment when he hit some of them that electrified people. In his early years it was the sheer power he displayed: the unbelievable length of his home runs. Players in that day simply didn't hit baseballs that far.

His first homer as a Major League professional was a case in point. It came in March, 1914, in Fayetteville, North Carolina, where

15

Ruth was at his first spring training camp with the then minor league Baltimore Orioles. It was the first game of the spring, an informal intrasquad affair in which the left-handed Ruth, a prize pitching prospect, played shortstop and another left-hander played second base (a left-handed double-play combination!). It was a nothing game, in other words, except for Ruth. Describing the action in the second inning, a Baltimore sportswriter covering spring training wrote, "The next batter made a hit that will live in the memory of all who saw it. That clouter was George Ruth, the southpaw from St. Mary's School. The ball carried so far to right field that he walked around the bases."

A year or two earlier Jim Thorpe, the famous Carlisle College Indian athlete, had hit a mammoth home run out of the Fayetteville ballpark that local people said was the longest ball ever hit there. Ruth's went sixty feet farther. It was stunning. Next day headlines in Baltimore newspapers shouted **RUTH MAKES MIGHTY CLOUT** and **HOMER BY RUTH FEATURE OF GAME**.

Home run headlines. He'd been a professional ballplayer less than a week.

During his first few seasons Ruth was a pitcher, and a great one. He was a power pitcher. Casey Stengel, who batted against him, said, "He had good stuff, a good fastball, a fine curve—a dipsy-do that made you think a little." As a member of the Boston Red Sox, from 1915 through 1918, the year he began his transition from the mound to the outfield, he won more games and had a lower earned run average than any other pitcher in the American League— except for the incomparable Walter Johnson— and he beat Johnson five straight times in mano-a-mano duels. After giving up a run in the first inning of the first World Series game he pitched (an inside-the-park homer hit by Henry "Hy" Myers), Ruth shut out Brooklyn for the

Twenty-year-old Babe Ruth in 1915 displays his pitching form as a member of the Boston Red Sox. His first Major League home run came that year in a game against...the Yankees.

16

next thirteen for a complete game 2–1 victory. He won two more games in the 1918 World Series, extending the consecutive scoreless inning streak to 29.

In those four pitching years with the Red Sox the Babe hit 20 home runs. Only three American League batters had more. Ty Cobb had fewer, only 18 during that same four-year period. Shoeless Joe Jackson had 14, George Sisler 11. It was astonishing for a pitcher to hit homers like that. And Ruth's blasts had a gargantuan impact, a buzz heard throughout baseball. His first big-league homer, on May 6, 1915, came in the old Polo Grounds in New York City, where Ruth was pitching for the Red Sox against the New York Yankees. This was long before Yankee Stadium. The Polo Grounds' foul lines were very short, but Ruth's clout carried far into the upper stands in right field, which in those days seemed a very long way from home plate. And he hit it "with no apparent effort," an admiring observer said.

When the Red Sox returned to the Polo Grounds in June, Ruth hit another homer, this one even longer than the first. Later that month in Fenway Park in Boston he hit one into the distant right-field bleachers, where only one ball had ever been hit before. In July in St. Louis he hit his fourth and last homer of the season (the league champion had seven), a ball that went completely out of the park in right, soared across a street, and broke a window in a building on the far side of the road. It was the longest home run ever seen in St. Louis up to that time.

In June of 1916, while pitching in Detroit, he hit his first home run of that year. In the next game the Red Sox played, in St. Louis, he pinch-hit with Boston losing 3–0 and hit a three-run homer "completely over the bleachers" to tie the score. The next day, pitching again and batting ninth, he had a perfect day at bat that included another home run—his third in three games—which created a sensation. Three home runs in three games!

Jackson had only three homers all year, Sisler four, Cobb five. Home runs were rare. Three in three games was phenomenal. Those were the only homers Ruth hit that season, but they were talked about all year.

He had only two in 1917, but both were memorable. In mid-season he hit the first homer ever into the center-field bleachers at Fenway. His second and last came in September before a crowd of newly inducted soldiers (the U.S. had entered World War I that year). The soldiers cheered Ruth loudly throughout the game, hoping to see a home run. Babe failed in his first two at-bats but in the sixth inning came close when he hit a tremendous fly ball foul over the right-field roof. In the ninth, in his final at-bat, with the soldiers beseeching him to hit one, he came through for them, lofting a ball into the right field seats.

By 1918 he was fed up with pitching and wanted to be a hitter full-time, but his manager, the crusty, old-fashioned Ed Barrow, was against the idea. After all, Ruth was his star pitcher. But in spring training the home run kept coming to the fore. Ruth hit two in the first exhibition game, hit five balls over the right-field fence in batting practice before a scheduled game at an army camp (the soldiers roared with glee each time a ball soared out of the park), hit a bases-loaded homer in the next game, and when he had only one hit, a single, in the following game a newspaper said, rather sadly, "Babe Ruth was not able to make any home runs."

When the Red Sox played another game at the army camp, Ruth, a pitcher and nothing else in Barrow's mind, was not in the lineup. The soldiers noisily demanded that he appear. Barrow reluctantly sent him into the game, and Babe hit a long homer in the eighth and a game-winning shot over the centerfielder's head in the ninth.

18   Yet he was still considered a pitcher, and not until a month into the 1918 season did Barrow finally begin to use him at first base and the outfield, as well as on the mound. Ruth responded with three home runs in three consecutive games in May, and a month later, after being hospitalized for a week with a throat infection, he hit four in four consecutive games.

By the end of June he had eleven homers, a spectacular number halfway through a season in that era, especially since the eleventh was a game-winning clout off Walter Johnson that put the Red Sox in first place.

Although he had just 20 career homers to this point, Ruth was called "The Home Run King." Even when he struck out it was impressive. A newspaper account said, "When Ruth misses a swipe at the ball, the stands quiver."

Pitching was now anathema for him. All spring he had resisted going to the mound, arguing that pitching and playing the field was too much for him. That led to repeated arguments with Barrow and finally an explosion. On July 2 Ruth jumped the club, saying he was quitting the Red Sox and would sign with an independent wartime baseball team sponsored by a Baltimore shipbuilder. That made great headlines for a day or two, but a peace between Ruth and Barrow was hammered out, and when wartime exigencies called for baseball to shut down a month early, Ruth agreed to pitch every fourth day and play the outfield the other three for the rest of the abbreviated season, which he did, batting fourth each day. He hit no more home runs, but he batted .300, won nine of his last eleven starts, and almost single-handedly led the Red Sox to the pennant and victory in the World Series. A Boston sportswriter wrote, "The more I see of Babe the more he seems a figure out of mythology."

In 1919 he became a full-time outfielder, although he still started fifteen games on the mound, and now his home runs became even bigger. Before the season began, playing in an exhibition game in Florida on a field laid out in the infield of a racetrack, Ruth hit an amazing homer, a ball that carried far over the right-fielder's head, beyond the rail and across the track. Sportswriters and others tried to measure the distance (was this the first "tape-measure" home run?). One version said it carried six hundred feet.

Barrow said 579 feet. The most conservative estimate was "more than 500 feet." All observers agreed it was the longest homer Ruth or anyone else had ever hit.

By now Ruth had made the home run famous. People marveled at his long, free swing, similar to Shoeless Joe Jackson's, although sportswriters were remarking on the similarity before Ruth ever saw Jackson play. Until Ruth came along, most hitters choked up a little on the bat and swung protectively—a strikeout was something of a disgrace—but Ruth disdained such caution. "I swing big," he said. It wasn't a muscular, crunchy swing, like Mark McGwire's, but graceful, loose, and flowing, deriving its power from perfect coordination rather than brute strength. "He had the prettiest swing of all," an admiring contemporary said.

In 1919, when he hit 29 to obliterate all previous single-season records, his home-run chase was reported in detailed, daily coverage.

19

Ruth and his "big swing."

nates baseball pedants and other nitpickers—whether or not Ruth actually pointed to a spot in center field and then hit the ball to that exact spot—absolutely begs the question, meaning it misses the point, if you'll forgive that pun.

Whether Ruth actually pointed portentously to a spot, as actors have done hammily in the various bad movies made about Ruth, doesn't matter. What matters is that in baseball's biggest show Ruth challenged the rival team and the rival crowd, both of which had been razzing him unmercifully all afternoon (lemons had been tossed at him during batting practice), and came through. When he batted in

22

the famous fifth inning the game was tied because of a grievous out-field miscue Ruth had made in the previous inning, which gave the Cub players and the Chicago fans even more reason for getting all over Ruth. Some players lose their composure when they suffer that sort of vocal abuse—Ruth had lost his more than once when he was a young player.

But now, secure in his accomplishments and confident of his ability (he was in his nineteenth big league season), he relished the moment. "That's the first time I ever got the players and the fans

Ruth, catcher, and umpire all watch as the ball leaves the yard during a game in 1934, his last year with the Yankees.

going at the same time," Ruth said later. "I never had so much fun in my life." He laughed at the razzing, smiled at the crowd, jeered the Cub bench in turn, waved a finger to invoke the old baseball axiom that it only takes one to hit it.

The implication was clear. When the irritated Chicago pitcher, Charlie Root, told him to stop futzing around and get in and hit, Ruth said cheerfully, "You put one in here and I'll knock it down your goddamn throat."

During all this did he actually point to an exact spot in the bleachers? Who cares? Under enormous pressure in the World Series, before a huge, heckling crowd, with the score tied, after indicating that he was going to hit one, he swung and drove a long, long home run to the most distant part of the center-field bleachers. The epic homer crushed the Cubs, crushed Chicago, delighted Governor Franklin D. Roosevelt of New York, who was running for President and was in the ballpark that afternoon, and put the Yankees ahead to stay as they went on to sweep the Series in four games.

Ruth finished his career with the Boston Braves in 1935. He was called "fat and old," but still was capable of awesome power. His 714th and last home run was hit completely out of Forbes Field in Pittsburgh; the distance was estimated at over 600 feet.

23

That's the drama of the called-shot home run, not whether or not he pointed to a precise spot. In the Yankee clubhouse after the game Ruth roared, "Did Mr. Ruth chase those guys back into the dugout? Mr. Ruth sure did!"

Earlier in that same game, loudly jeered in the first inning while waiting to bat, Ruth grinned at the bench jockeys on the step of the Cubs' dugout and pointed to the right-field bleachers. When he batted a few moments later he hit a three-run homer into those bleachers. That was a called-shot home run the pedants and nitpickers don't seem much interested in.

Ruth himself said, "I used to pop off a lot about hitting homers. I'd say, 'Okay, you bums. I'll hit one!' Sometimes I did. Sometimes I didn't. Hell, it was fun."

In some ways Ruth's greatest moment came in 1935, when he was about through as a ballplayer. His home runs over the previous three

24

The Great Bambino as a Yankee old-timer in 1942.

seasons had declined from 41 to 34 to 22 and his batting average from .341 to .301 to .288, his lowest since 1916. The Yankees let him go and he signed with the old Boston Braves for a last hurrah. But he played poorly, realized he was washed up, and decided to retire after one final road trip. By the time the club reached Pittsburgh, his batting average was hovering around .150, and he had hit but three home runs. But in the last game in Pittsburgh, rising like a wounded lion for one desperate assault, Ruth staged a majestic grand finale to his glorious career. He had four hits in four at-bats and batted in six runs. He hit a two-run homer in the first inning, another two-run homer in the third inning, a run-scoring single in the fifth, and in the seventh, with the bases empty, hit a third home run, this one the first ball ever hit over the right-field roof and out of old Forbes Field. It landed on the roof of a house. The Pirates' head usher later measured the distance from the house back to home plate and said it was 600 feet. The measurement may have been inaccurate but everyone agreed it was the longest homer ever hit at Forbes Field.

It was also Ruth's 714th and last home run, his last hit. He appeared briefly in a few more games and then packed it in.

The pitcher Ruth hit his last two home runs off was Guy Bush, a Major Leaguer for more than fifteen years, whose memory of Babe's final homer can serve as an epitaph for Ruth as home run hitter. Bush said, "I never saw a ball hit so hard before or since. He was fat and old, but he still had that great swing. Even when he missed, you could hear the bat go *swish*. I can't remember anything about the first home run he hit off me. I guess it was just another homer. But I can't forget that last one. It's probably still going."

during the nine seasons from 1955 through 1963, he missed just sixteen games. For Henry Aaron there were no career deprivations, no vaporous musings of "What if?" Year after year he took full advantage of his opportunities, using every resource of his talent with record-shattering consistency of power hitting.

There is no way to break baseball's Valhalla records other than through consistency. That was how Pete Rose finally moved Ty Cobb aside as the all-time hit leader. Rose did it, for the most part, with singles and doubles; for Aaron, the climb to the summit was more difficult. A base hit can be achieved with a bunt or through a bad hop. Mathematically, a .250 hitter averages roughly as many hits as games. But a home run . . .

When he retired from active play, Henry Aaron joked, "I don't have to worry about the curve ball anymore." The comment must have amused the National League pitchers he had tormented for more than twenty years, who probably found it hard to imagine Aaron every worrying about *anything* up at home plate. In the batter's box, he exuded a calm that bordered on disinterest. "It was confidence," said Bobby Bragan, one of his managers, "that's what that was, and as intense a concentration as I have ever seen in a hitter. He didn't light up a field the way a Mays or a Clemente did, but he was their equal. Willie got all the attention—and he deserved it—but Henry did it longer. And in the opinion of a lot of people he did it just as well if not better."

Henry Louis Aaron was born in Mobile, Alabama, on February 5, 1934. Aaron was born three years after that vintage year for home run hitters, 1931, which saw the births of Ernie Banks, Willie Mays, Mickey Mantle, and Aaron's future teammate Eddie Mathews, all of whom hit over 500 career home runs.

One of eight children, Henry was a quiet youngster who early in life demonstrated an insatiable passion for baseball. It was a familiar story in the childhood tales of future stars: the desire animated the talent and the talent quickened the desire. It's been said that from the time he was four years old until he left home in 1951 at the age of seventeen to play for the Indianapolis Clowns of the Negro American League, Aaron played baseball virtually every day of his life.

A talent the size and quality of Henry Aaron's soon becomes its

28

Wearing number 5, Aaron as a rookie for the Milwaukee Braves in 1954.

own skyline. In 1952 Boston Braves scout Dewey Griggs saw Aaron play in Buffalo and sent back a most unambiguous report. "Aaron," said Griggs, "is one of the finest hitters God ever put on this earth. I don't know what it would take to get this guy, but I'd pay it out of my own pocket." The Braves moved without delay and secured an option on Aaron, at virtually the same time the New York Giants sent the young man a contract.

"I had the contract in my hand," Aaron said later, "but the Braves offered fifty dollars more a month to play at Eau Claire in the Class C Northern League than the Giants offered at Sioux City in the Class A Western League. That's the only thing that kept Willie Mays and me from being teammates—fifty dollars."

And that's one for baseball fans to tantalize themselves with on sleepless nights—Mays and Aaron in the same field for the next sixteen or so years, hitting all of those home runs in tandem.

Aaron, a shortstop then, hit .336 for Eau Claire in 87 games, with 9 home runs. His 35 errors prompted the Braves to move him to second base when they promoted him to their Jacksonville, Florida club in the Class A Sally League in 1953. At Jacksonville, Aaron flourished, hitting a respectable 22 home runs (second highest in the league) and leading the league in batting, hits, runs batted in, runs, and doubles. As a reward for this cannonade he was invited to the Milwaukee Braves' spring training camp in 1954, though the club had already ticketed him for another year in the minors, at the AAA level. Thanks to a caprice of fate that spring, Aaron's career took a quantum leap forward.

Deciding that they needed another right-handed power bat, the Braves had acquired outfielder Bobby Thomson from the New York Giants on February 1, 1954. The man who had struck baseball's most resonant home run three years earlier was still in the prime of a solid career. The Braves believed he would help balance a lineup that featured the lethal left-handed bat of twenty-two-year-old Eddie Mathews, who had erupted to stardom the year before with a league-leading 47 home runs.

On March 13, 1954, in a preseason game at St. Petersburg, Thomson broke his ankle sliding into second base. With the team's new acquisition gone for most of the season—Thomson didn't return to the active roll until August 22—Braves manager Charlie Grimm had a gaping hole in his lineup. To fill it he turned to Henry Aaron. Not only was the twenty-year-old being jumped to the big leagues, but

29

he was given a position he had never played professionally—left field. (Later he moved to right field, where he played most of his career.)

On April 23, 1954 in St. Louis, the rookie outfielder hit his first big league home run, off veteran right-hander Vic Raschi.

"Years later," Raschi, one-time ace of the New York Yankees staff, said, "my phone began to ring. Aaron was closing in on Ruth's all-time home run record and everybody wanted to know about that first one, way back in 1954. I felt like the guy with the bottle of champagne who launches the battleship and sends it on its way. I guess you might say I launched Hank Aaron. One newspaperman wanted to know what kind of pitch it was. Well, I didn't even know who Henry Aaron was at the time, much less what kind of pitch he'd hit. But one thing I did notice about the kid, and that was how quick his wrists were."

Those wrists. That was what everyone marveled at. How quick and how strong. They enabled him to withhold his swing until the last split second. "Even if you managed to fool him with a pitch," Dodgers catcher Roy Campanella said, "he was still quick enough with those wrists to adjust. I swear he hit pitches right over my glove."

30   Unlike such muscular contemporaries such as Ted Kluszewski, Harmon Killebrew, Frank Howard, and others, Aaron was trim of build and did not project an aura of brute strength.

"He was pretty strong through the shoulders and arms," Dodgers manager Walter Alston said. "But the thing that made Aaron the hitter that he was, was his timing and those powerful wrists. You see,

Aaron and his "powerful wrists."

when he made contact with the ball it was at the precise moment when those wrists were rolling over or snapping. He never looked like he was attacking the ball, like most heavy hitters do. He held the bat up and away from his body and just seemed to flick it, but those wrists generated terrific bat speed and he hit the ball very hard."

There was no indication in the beginning that Aaron was going to become a home run hitter, much less the game's most prolific. He played 122 games in that rookie 1954 season, batting .280 and hitting a modest 13 home runs. On September 5 he broke his ankle sliding into third base—the only serious injury of his long career—ironically, the pinch-runner was Bobby Thomson.

In the next two seasons Aaron hit 27 and then 26 home runs, respectable numbers but nowhere near the totals being amassed by National League busters like Mays, Kluszewski, Ernie Banks, Duke Snider, and Aaron's lineup mate, Eddie Mathews. A year later, however, Aaron exploded with a league-leading 44 home runs (the first of four times he was to hit that exact number), beating out Banks by one. It was Aaron's breakout year to high stardom. The year before, his .328 batting average had earned him the first of his two batting titles, and now that deadly snap of the swing gave him the first of his four home run crowns, plus a league-leading 132 runs batted in, earning him the Most Valuable Player award.

It was toward the end of the 1957 season that Aaron achieved

31

A jubilant Hank Aaron is carried off the field after his eleventh-inning home run gave the Milwaukee Braves a 4–2 win over the St. Louis Cardinals and the 1957 National League pennant.

something that seduces the thoughts of every baseball-dreamy youngster. The Braves (who had lost the pennant the year before to the Brooklyn Dodgers by a heartbreaking single game) held a five-game lead over the Cardinals with six left to play. The Cardinals came to Milwaukee for a three-game series, needing to sweep to stay alive, while the Braves needed a single win to end it. The first game went to the eleventh inning tied at 2–2. Right-hander Lew Burdette held off the Cardinals in the top of the eleventh; in the bottom half of the inning the Braves leadoff man walked, bringing Aaron to the plate.

For Aaron the quintessential home run had always been Bobby Thomson's resounding 1951 wallop. "I used to think about that shot," Aaron said. "That had always been my idea of the most important homer."

On the first pitch from Cardinal reliever Billy Muffett, Aaron snapped those steel-spring wrists and drove the ball over the center-field fence, giving the Braves their first pennant and Henry Aaron one of those rare, special home runs. "Now I had one for myself," he said. It would always remain his most important home run.

Forty-four home runs, including a pennant-winner, and then three more in the Braves' seven-game World Series win over the Yankees.

"To tell you the truth," Alston said, "I never thought he'd be the home run hitter he became. He'd pop them all right, but they never went any farther than they had to; it was like he measured off the distance that he needed before the game and that's how far he'd hit them."

32

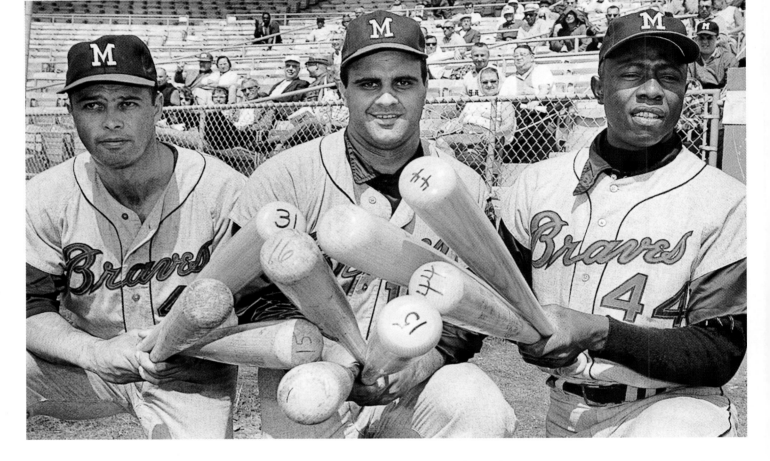

Economy of distance. A curious concept when associated with baseball's greatest home run hitter. Ralph Kiner, one of the game's premier long-ballers, said in 1975, "When people talk about home run hitters, the landmark names are Babe Ruth, Jimmie Foxx, Mickey Mantle, Ted Williams—the men who could put that ball out there a long way. Ironically, you don't often hear mentioned the name of Hank Aaron, and the reason for that is simple: Hank as a rule does not hit for tremendous distance; he hits steadily and well, but it's that long ball, that five-hundred-foot clout, which seems to capture the imagination of the fans."

So Henry Aaron was the most numerically successful home run hitter not mentioned among the game's signature home run hitters. There was another reason for this other than Aaron's not hitting the

Three heavy hitters for the 1965 Milwaukee Braves display their lumber. Left to right, Eddie Mathews, Joe Torre, and Hank Aaron.

ball for prodigious distances. "Hammerin'
Hank" never challenged a single-season home
run record, not Ruth's 60 nor Hack Wilson's
National League mark of 56. His high-water
mark was 47, in 1971, and even then he was
aced by Willie Stargell's 48. His second-best
was 45, in 1962, and Willie Mays topped him
with 49. Only once did he hit three home
runs in a game, on June 21, 1959, in San
Francisco, against the Giants.

When it comes to records for leading in
home runs, or for most home runs in a given
month or week, or for most multiple home
run games in a season or career, or for consecutive games, or for grand slams, Hank
Aaron's name is not to be found.

Aaron achieved his record-setting home run total not with spectacular home plate fireworks but with a two-decade-long display of
extraordinary high-powered consistency. Look for Aaron's name in
the home run record columns and you will find, in addition to his
snow-capped career total, entries for National League record for most
years with 40 or more home runs (8), Major League record for
most years with 30 or more home runs (15), Major League record
for most consecutive years with 20 or more home runs (20).

Aaron was a long distance runner with a spectacular kick.
Beginning in 1969, at the age of thirty-five, his home run totals were

*(Above) Aaron accepting
congratulations from
Eddie Mathews and the
Braves bat boy after
hitting his 399th home
run against the
Philadelphia Phillies
on April 20, 1966.*

33

*(Left) Two views of Aaron
as he connects on his
600th home run on April
28, 1971 in Atlanta.*

44, 38, 47, 34, and 40, a five-year total of 203 for a yearly average of 40.6. Beginning at the same age, Ruth's five-year total was 192 for an average of 38.4, while Mays hit but 123, averaging 24.6 per year.

When the thirty-nine-year-old Mays ended the 1970 season with 628 hammer shots, sportswriters speculated about his chances of overtaking Ruth. Aaron had completed the season with 592.

"Guys kept writing about Willie's chances," Aaron said later, "but I was always wondering about mine. Truthful, though, the first time I really thought I might challenge Ruth was in 1971. I had expected my homer production to slow down, but when I hit 47 that year I knew I had a chance."

With the dogged consistency that was to become the hallmark of his career, he concluded the 1972 season with 673 home runs, entering a rarefied atmosphere that only Ruth had passed through. And then, in 1973, like a man zealously dedicated to the work at hand, he turned in what was statistically the most torrid long-ball season. The thirty-nine-year-old Aaron started in a little over a hundred games, came to bat just 392 times, and delivered a remarkable 40 home runs—an average of 10.2 homers per 100 at-bats, the highest of his career. Think of a man, after a long and arduous climb, suddenly sprinting to the top of Everest. It left his career mark at a tantalizing 713, one short of Ruth's—a difference he was to erase with two quick and efficient swings early in 1974.

34

(Above) The home run chase is on! On July 22, 1973, Aaron reads the story of his 700th home run, just 14 from tying Babe Ruth's seemingly insurmountable record.

(Left) The two home run kings compare stances. On the left, Japanese slugger Sadaharu Oh and on the right, in his leisurely best, Hank Aaron.

(Opposite) April 8, 1974, after connecting off Los Angeles Dodgers pitcher Al Downing, Aaron watches and knows that he has just become a baseball immortal.

What are the thoughts of the greatest home run hitter of all time?

What Aaron achieved, finally, was to clear the mists of legend from that long-magic and supposedly unconquerable 714 and give a new generation of baseball fans their own witnessed and experienced legend of 755. Henry Aaron in a sense modernized baseball greatness, while expanding the perimeters of athletic achievement. He is the architect of the tallest building, and we can only wait and see if someone can do better.

HEIRS TO THE THRONE

Babe Ruth retired in 1935, his lifetime total of 714 home runs seemingly secure in the record books, one of the game's "unbreakable" records. But no word in the baseball lexicon has become more misapplied.

Ruth's record lasted until early in the 1974 season—nearly forty years. Will Aaron's 755 remain the standard for that many years?

Ken Griffey, Jr. The heir apparent?

At the close of the century, twenty-five years after establishing his record, Aaron can begin to distinguish challengers on the horizon. Foremost among the latter are Mark McGwire and Ken Griffey, Jr. While age may be against McGwire (he turned thirty-six years old on October 1, 1999), he did finish the 1999 season with 522 home runs, leaving him 234 away from a new record. To pass Aaron, he would have to do what he did from 1996–99: average nearly 60 home runs a year for four more years. Impossible? Well, dare we use that word when speaking of the man who hit 70?

During a visit to Seattle in 1999, Aaron said jokingly to Griffey, "Slow down a bit, won't you?" On April 10, 2000, Griffey, 30 years old, hit his 400th home run, the youngest major leaguer to reach that mark, leaving him 356 away from breaking the record. From 1996–99, Griffey averaged 53 one-way shots per season. If he plays another nine years, he needs to average 40 home runs per season to pass Aaron. Barring injury, baseball could well be crowning a new all-time home run champion sometime during the new century's first decade. The odds are his name will be Ken Griffey, Jr.

The
500 Club

Berry Stainback

It's an elite club. A club with, as of spring 2000, only sixteen members. But though the membership is limited, the club is open to anyone skilled enough to meet the one very strict requirement: 500 or more home runs in a career. The sixteen members of the 500 Club are a diverse group. Some are big and lumbering, others are tall and lean. A few played in the first half of the twentieth century while the rest hit their home runs after World War II. What all the members have in common is consistency. To hit 500 or more home runs in a career

(Opposite) Banks doffing his cap to the fans as he crosses the plate after hitting his 500th home run on May 12, 1970.

39

The two highest ranking members of the 500 Club: Hank Aaron and Babe Ruth.

requires season after season of home run production. There can be no long term slumps. There can be no lengthy injuries. The numbers have to be there on a regular basis or the chances of joining the club diminish rapidly.

The achievements of the two 500 Club leaders, Hank Aaron at 755 and Babe Ruth at 714, have already been documented here. What follows is, in order of the number of home runs they hit, the rest of the 500 Club roster.

WILLIE MAYS *660*

Willie joined the New York Giants at age nineteen and he played baseball with an uninhibited joy and unrestrained abandon. Whether he was making diving catches in center field, nailing base runners with his strong, accurate arm, or stealing second and coming up with a grin on his face, people watching him invariably did so with smiles on their faces. In his early years Mays would leave the Polo Grounds and play stickball with kids in the streets of Harlem.

(Left) The "Say Hey" Kid demonstrating the proper way to tape a bat to a young fan at the opening of the New York Giants 1956 spring training season.

For more than ten years Mays was the finest all-around player in the game. On defense he won the Gold Glove twelve times and finished his career with more outfield putouts than any man in history. On the basepaths he could steal almost any time his team needed him to. He hit for average and he hit with power, even though he was not regarded as a slugger on the order of Mickey Mantle.

Yet Mays led the National League in home runs four times, starting in 1955 with 51 and ending ten years later with 52. But Willie found many ways to beat his opponents. Consider his play in the 1963 All-Star Game. Although he had only one single in three at-bats, he stole two bases, scored twice, and drove in two runs in the NL victory. Afterward, manager Alvin Dark said, "That Willie always finds a way to win. If you were stuck somewhere in China, he'd come up with a rickshaw."

(Below) Willie Mays in action in 1969.

40

FRANK ROBINSON *586*

Robinson, who played from 1956 through 1976, was a throwback to the days of Ty Cobb. With Robinson on first base, there was no such thing as a routine force play. He always slid hard and knocked the infielder on his butt. He wanted opponents to worry about him. At bat he crowded the plate, taking the inside away from the pitcher and protecting the outside corner. When the pitcher released the ball, Robinson would dive into it. If the pitch was inside, his wrists were so strong he could pull the ball. If the pitch was outside, he could power it to right. He was amazingly quick at spinning away from inside pitches. Yet in each of his ten years in the National League, Robinson was hit by more pitched balls than any other player.

Robinson recalls one manager who told his pitchers, "I want you to hit Frank Robinson as soon as he walks out of the dugout."

But nothing stopped Frank Robinson from challenging opponents. Robinson would be hit in the head, throw away his cracked batting helmet, and play the next day. He did anything to win, even when he was injured and unable to swing the bat well.

Typical was his performance in an extra-inning game his Orioles were playing in Boston. Robinson had severely bruised his back when he made a game-saving catch by crashing into the right-field wall. In the bottom of the inning he came up with the bases loaded and beat out a bunt to win the game.

Robinson was named the NL Most Valuable Player after he led the Cincinnati Reds to the pennant in 1961. Less than five years later he was called "an old thirty" by Reds owner Bill DeWitt and traded to the Orioles. So Robinson won the Triple Crown—leading the AL in hitting, RBIs, and home runs with 49—and went on to earn MVP honors in the Orioles' World Series victory over the Dodgers. He was also the league's MVP—the only man ever named the most valuable player in both leagues.

Frank Robinson receives a firm handshake from sleeveless Ted Kluszewski after crossing home plate on his 38th home run of the year against the New York Giants at the Polo Grounds on September 11, 1956. With the homer, Robinson equalled the Major League home run record for a first-year player set by Wally Berger of the 1930 Boston Braves.

41

42

Robinson, shown here displaying his stroke in 1966, was called an "old thirty" when he was traded from the Cincinnati Reds to the Baltimore Orioles prior to that season. "Old" Frank Robinson went on to win the American League Triple Crown that year and lead the Orioles to a World Series victory. And that trade is now known as one of the most lopsided in Major League Baseball history.

HARMON KILLEBREW 573

One writer said, "Everything about him suggested the characteristics of the humble apple, the state fruit of his native Idaho. Modest, unassuming, self-effacing, folksy." He might just be the shyest of the 500 Club members. But he could also be the strongest. At 5'11" and 205 pounds, Killebrew inherited his physique from his grandfather, Harmon C. Killebrew, a Civil War strongman. He was built like a blacksmith, with a thick chest and powerful arms. And when he connected with a baseball it traveled miles.

"Folksy" Harmon Killebrew in 1965.

43

Killebrew began his career at seventeen with the Washington Senators in 1954. He played sparingly, moving back and forth from the minors to the majors until 1959, when Senators owner Cal Griffith ordered his manager to play the youngster at third base. Killebrew promptly hit 15 home runs in May. So opposing pitchers began knocking him down. That annoyed Killebrew, who would get up, dust himself off, and hit another home run. "Getting a chance to play gave me more confidence," he said. "I wasn't going for so many bad pitches."

Killebrew bashes his 500th home run in a game against the Baltimore Orioles in 1971.

He finished the season with a league-leading 42 home runs. His homers fell to 31 the next year, but in 1961 the team moved from massive Griffith Stadium to Metropolitan Stadium in Minneapolis, which was only 330 feet down each foul line. Killebrew could stroke high fly balls that would clear the Met fences. He hit 29 of his 46 four-baggers at home, though few of the Killer's homers were cheap shots.

He led the league in home runs five more times, in 1962 (with 48), '63 (45), '64 (49), '67 (44) and '69 (49). His biggest asset as a hitter was his ability to smash a pitcher's best pitch. The low outside pitch is the most difficult for any pull-hitter to handle. Steve Hamilton of the Yankees said, "I threw him the perfect pitch low and away, but Killebrew went out and hit it over the right-field fence. That's what I call overpowering the ball." The humble Killer could do that.

REGGIE JACKSON 563

In a career that began in 1967 and ended twenty years later in 1987, Reggie Jackson was driven by an ego that would not allow him to do anything but excel. In 1968, his first full season, Jackson hit 29 homers for the Athletics, who had just moved from Kansas City to Oakland. The next year, he stunned the baseball world by clubbing 47 home runs. That was a season's total he would never again top, and his strikeout total often surpassed the number of games he appeared in. But nothing diminished Jackson's exalted view of himself.

For example, after he accumulated only 23 homers and a .237 batting average in 1970, he said, "I'll come back strong next year." He did, bringing his average up to .277 and hitting 32 home runs. He slipped again in '72, hitting only 25 home runs. "You'll see the real Reggie in '73," he said. And he produced a league-leading 32 homers and drove in 117, which earned him the AL's Most Valuable Player Award. He also starred in the World Series against the Mets. Although the A's hit no home runs off the sparkling New York pitching through six games, Reggie's three hits off Tom Seaver won that game to tie the Series. Then Jackson sealed the victory in the final game with a two-run homer off Jon Matlack. He won Series MVP honors.

For his heroics, Jackson began calling himself Mr. October, suggesting that his clutch-hitting prowess made the World Series month his. In 1977 he signed with the New York Yankees. A number of his new teammates had trouble understanding Jackson and his supreme ego. But pitcher Catfish Hunter, who had played with

Young Reggie Jackson kicks up dirt as he takes a mighty cut in a game in 1969. In that season, his second full one in the Majors, Jackson stroked a whopping 47 homers.

44

Mr. October tips his cap to the fans at Yankee Stadium from his position in right field in the top of the ninth inning of game six of the 1977 World Series. In the previous inning, Jackson had just connected on his third consecutive home run to cap the Yankees, 8–4 defeat of the Los Angeles Dodgers, clinching the 1977 World Series.

45

Jackson on the A's, explained what people didn't understand about the right fielder. "Reggie wants everybody to love him," Catfish said. Jackson did his best to make them do just that in the Yankees' victories over the Dodgers in the 1977 and '78 World Series. He hit seven home runs and drove in 16 in those two Series including the famous three in game six of the 1977 Series. What else would you expect from Mr. October?

Big Bats

The equipment a slugger uses to ply his trade is as important to him as the swing he employs. They each go hand in hand. Like Roy Hobbs in *The Natural*, he is deemed powerless without his Wonderboy. Here are some of the Wonderboys, and their weight and length, used by five members of the 500 Club.

The bat (and the ball) used by Mark McGwire in hitting his 62nd home run in 1998.

Babe Ruth	Louisville Slugger 125	35 inches	35 ounces
Ted Williams	Louisville Slugger 125	35 inches	32 ounces
Reggie Jackson	Rawlings Adirondack 302	34.5 inches	32 ounces
Mike Schmidt	Rawlings Adirondack 302	35 inches	32 ounces
Mark McGwire	Rawlings Adirondack 302*	35 inches	32 ounces

Though the logo on the barrel changed from "Rawlings" to an "R" in a circle, McGwire has used the same manufacturer and model from 1987 to the present.

MIKE SCHMIDT 548

Mike Schmidt joined the Philadelphia Phillies at age twenty-two as a power-hitting third baseman. He had a big swing at the plate and a wild arm throwing from third base. His swings for the seats often resulted in strikeouts and his throws to first base all too often found the seats. Notoriously impatient Phillie fans booed the rookie incessantly. Yet manager Danny Ozark stuck with Schmidt, and Mike ignored the fans. In 1974, though still striking out too much, Mike Schmidt led the league in home runs. By the time he retired early

in the 1989 season, Schmidt had made himself into a slick-fielding defensive player and hit more than any other third baseman in baseball history.

Schmidt was the National League home run leader from 1974 through '76. In 1980, his Phillies met the Expos on the next-to-last day of the season to decide the pennant. Although the Phillies made five errors in the game, they won on an eleventh-inning homer off the bat of Schmidt. Next, the surprising Phillies beat the Astros in the playoffs and went on to defeat the Kansas City Royals in the World Series.

Schmidt was named the league's MVP in 1980 on the strength of 48 home runs—a record for a third baseman—and 121 RBIs. He repeated as MVP in the strike-shortened '81 season, which he led with 31 homers, 91 RBIs, 78 runs scored, and a slugging percentage of .644. Although the Phillies could not continue their winning ways, Schmidt continued to excel, and in 1986 he led the National League in home runs (37) and in runs batted in (119). Schmidt finished his career with ten Gold Gloves, ten All-Star Game appearances, and an NL-record eight home run crowns.

(Left) Mike Schmidt, the top home run hitter of the decade of the 1980s.

47

(Left) Schmidt watches his 535th home run disappear into the night in a game against the San Diego Padres in 1988. The home run moved Schmidt past Jimmie Foxx on the all-time home run list.

MICKEY MANTLE 536

Mickey Mantle takes a right-handed pre-game swing in 1961, the year he hit an impressive 54 homers only to take a back seat to Roger Maris, who hit 61 the same year.

48

In 1951, at age nineteen, Mickey Mantle went to spring training with the Yankees, and manager Casey Stengel said, "That young fellow has me terribly confused. He should have a year in Triple A ball but. . . ." But that young fellow hit the ball out of the park from both sides of the plate and he ran to first base in an unheard of 3.1 seconds. Playing next to center fielder Joe DiMaggio, Mantle opened the season in right field.

Plagued by strikeouts, on July 15 he was sent down to triple A. He thought about quitting until the father he idolized told him, "If that's all the courage you have, go ahead and quit." Mantle drove in 50 runs in 40 games for the Triple A team, then returned to the Yankees. And the rest is an amazing bit of history, because by all rights Mantle should not even have been playing baseball. He had osteomyelitis—a persistent inflammation of the bone marrow—in his right leg. Adding to his chronically bad knees, in the 1951 World Series he stepped in an outfield drain and tore cartilage in his right knee. He would suffer untold injuries throughout his career. Yet for more than ten years Mickey Mantle was the dominant player in baseball.

In 1956 he became only the sixth man in AL history to win the Triple Crown, with a batting average of .353, 52 home runs, and 130

runs batted in. He also scored 132 runs and was named MVP. He repeated as MVP the next year when he raised his batting average to .365, hit 34 home runs, and drove in 94. In '62 he won yet another MVP award and led the Yankees to their tenth pennant in his twelve years with the club. Despite constant injuries, Mantle gutted it out for six more years before finally retiring after the 1968 season, ending his career as the most powerful switch-hitter ever to play the game.

(Left) The two 1957 MVPs cross bats: Mantle, the American League winner, and Hank Aaron, his National League counterpart. This photo was taken at a home run hitting contest in 1958.

(Below) Mantle's 501st home run, May 18, 1967, captured in sequence.

49

JIMMIE FOXX 534

Called "Double X," baseball insiders regarded him as the right-handed-hitting Babe Ruth of the 1930s. The six-foot, 195-pound Foxx is the only man ever to hit 30 or more home runs in twelve consecutive seasons.

He broke in with Connie Mack's Philadelphia A's in 1925. His gargantuan power shots helped them win three straight pennants begin-

(Left) Jimmie Foxx in his last season, 1945, as a member of the Philadelphia Phillies.

(Below) Foxx showing his Philadelphia Athletics manager, Connie Mack, his favorite tools during a spring training session in 1931.

ning in 1929. He hit 33 home runs and batted .354 in '29, followed by a 37-homer, 156-RBI season, and a 30-homer, 120-RBI season. In the three World Series Foxx slugged four home runs, drove in 11, and had a .609 slugging percentage.

But it was in 1932 that Foxx lifted the home-run crown from Ruth's head for the first time since 1925. Ruth hit 41 homers, but Foxx hit 58, coming within two of the Babe's 1927 Major League record. Although the A's fell to second place, Foxx was named the AL's Most Valuable Player.

In 1936 Foxx and three of his teammates were traded to the Red Sox. Double X had five solid seasons in Boston, hitting in successive years 41 home runs, 36, 50, 35, and 36 before age began to catch up with him. Yet when his career ended after the 1945 season, Jimmie Foxx had joined the distinguished company of Ruth and Lou Gehrig as the only men to drive in over 100 runs in thirteen seasons.

50

MARK MCGWIRE 522

Mark McGwire reported to the Oakland Athletics as a 6′5″, 215-pound rookie in 1987 and immediately made a large impact on the game. In that year he slugged 49 home runs—a record for a first-year player—and was named Rookie of the Year.

Baseball people predicted that big Mark, a quiet, retiring individual, would go on to win a lot of home run titles before he was finished. No one could foresee that McGwire would have to be placed on the disabled list eight times in the first ten years of his career, often with a bad back.

It was not until nine years after his rookie season that McGwire would again become a home run champion, in 1996, when he hit 52. But the very next season, at age thirty-three, he was traded to the St. Louis Cardinals in July, even though he had already powered 34 home runs for the A's. When he added 24 for the Cards he became the first player ever to accumulate more than 20 home runs for two teams in the same season.

Yet in 1998 McGwire truly shocked the baseball world by surpassing the single-season home run records of both Babe Ruth (60) and Roger Maris (61). Mark hit 70. He engaged in a furious homer race with Sammy Sosa of the Cubs that resumed in '99 with McGwire hitting 65 and Sosa 63. It was in 1999 that McGwire also joined the elite 500 Club, thus making him the only active player to be a member of the club.

(Above) Mark McGwire flexes his brawny forearms as a member of the Oakland Athletics.

51

(Left) McGwire, with the Cardinals, watches his 500th home run sail over the fence on August 5, 1999.

TED WILLIAMS *521*

At age nineteen, Ted Williams had only a year and a half of minor league ball under his bat when he went to spring training with the Red Sox in 1938. Bobby Doerr, age nineteen, said to Ted, "Wait till you see Jimmie Foxx hit!" Williams snapped back, "Wait'll Foxx sees me hit!" Williams quickly became known as The Kid. He didn't care much for defensive play as a youngster and at times sat down in the outfield during games. But at the plate, no one was ever more serious than The Kid. Nobody practiced swinging a bat at a baseball more than Williams did. Many called Williams a natural hitter as a result of his smooth, swift, flawless swing and his rare vision that tested in the Naval Reserve at 20/10. But to his vision and swing you have to add the fact that Williams constantly studied pitchers. The Kid could tell you the name and location of every pitch that was ever thrown to him.

Small wonder then that Williams became, in the view of most experts, the greatest all-around hitter in baseball history. He is the last man to hit .400 or above, a feat he accomplished in 1941 when he also compiled a slugging percentage of .735. In the more than fifty years since Williams batted .406, the man who came closest to that average between 1941 and 1977 was The Kid himself when, in l958, he batted .388—at age thirty-eight. Six times Williams led the league in hitting. Pitchers so feared him that he regularly led the league in walks. He made the All-Star team eighteen times.

Williams, who hit a fabled homer in his last at-bat, always said, "When I finish my career I want people to point at me and say, 'There goes the greatest hitter who ever lived!'" The Kid got his wish.

52

(Left) Ted Williams in 1941, the year he batted .406.

(Below) Williams's "smooth, swift, flawless swing."

WILLIE MCCOVEY *521*

A tall, long-ball-hitting first baseman, Willie McCovey would have started the 1959 season with the San Francisco Giants . . . except the club had the '58 Rookie of the Year, Orlando Cepeda, playing first. When McCovey was brought up in midseason, he played the final 51 games at first and Cepeda switched to the outfield. McCovey, who was called Stretch, hit 13 home runs in only 192 at-bats, drove in 38 runs, and compiled a .354 batting average. He was the Giants' new Rookie of the Year.

(Above) Willie "Stretch" McCovey.

Playing in an average of less than 100 games per year the next three seasons, many as a pinch hitter, McCovey still slugged 51 home runs over those three years. The Giants had to make him a regular in '63. McCovey drove in 102 runs and hit a league-leading 44 home runs. He became the most feared left-handed power hitter in the NL. With Cepeda sidelined by a knee injury in '65 (and traded the following year), Stretch became the Giants' regular first baseman. He hit 39 home runs and drove in 92.

From 1965 through 1970 McCovey never hit fewer than 31 home runs or drove in less than 91 runs. His career year came in 1969 when he clubbed 45 home runs, had 126 RBIs, and a slugging percentage of .656. He was named the league's Most Valuable Player.

In the 1970s injuries reduced McCovey's playing time as he moved from San Francisco to San Diego, where he played three seasons, and, after a brief stint in Oakland, returned to the Giants in 1977. Back home, he celebrated at age thirty-nine by hitting 28 home runs and winning Comeback Player of the Year recognition. When Willie McCovey retired in 1980, he had hit 142 more home runs than his friend, Orlando Cepeda.

53

(Below) Tall and lean, McCovey hitting a home run as a rookie for the San Francisco Giants in 1959.

EDDIE MATHEWS *512*

54

Eddie Mathews always maintained that he was lucky to bat behind Henry Aaron. But this was not so in their early years together. Mathews joined the Braves in their last season in Boston, 1952, and hit 25 home runs. The following year the club moved to Milwaukee and the left-handed-hitting third baseman stroked 47 home runs to lead the league.

The next season twenty-year-old Hank Aaron joined the Braves, and Mathews hit 40 home runs. In 1955 he hit 41. It was not until the '57 season that Hammering Hank outpowered Mathews with a league-leading 44 home runs. In '59 it was Mathews's turn to win the NL home run title when he hit 46 (Aaron had 39). After the team moved to Atlanta, the two of them went on to finish their careers with a combined total of sixty more home runs than the famed Ruth-Gehrig duo: 1,267.

Mathews took pride in his fine play at third base and in his keen eye at the plate which allowed him to lead the league in walks four times. But in the end he bowed to Aaron when it came to hitting. "Playing with the Hammer definitely helped my career," Mathews said. "I usually batted behind Hank and if the pitcher got him out, he was so tired from the effort he might make a mistake with me."

"Playing with the Hammer [Hank Aaron] definitely helped my career," said Eddie Mathews, shown here probably watching Aaron, who usually batted in front of him, clout one.

ERNIE BANKS *512*

The man known as Mr. Cub during his nineteen years with Chicago was tall (6′1″) but slender to the point of being skinny. How did he accumulate 512 home runs? He had wrists of steel or, as pitcher Robin Roberts said, "From the elbows down he has the muscles of a 230-pounder."

In his first full season with the Cubs (1954) Banks hit 19 home runs, a nice total for a shortstop. He used a 35-ounce bat; the area you could get a hit on was about the size of a half-dollar. The next year he switched to a 31-ounce bat and the "hit" area shrunk to about the size of a dime. No problem. "Man, I could really swish that little stick," Banks said of the lighter length of ash.

Swishing that little stick in '55, Banks—who had never hit a grand slam home run—hit five of them, breaking a record shared by Ruth, Gehrig, Hank Greenberg, and Ralph Kiner. Banks hit 44 homers that

(Above) Mr. Cub, Ernie Banks, in 1955, the year he hit 44 home runs.

55

(Left) Ernie Banks displays the number of grand slams he hit in 1955.

year. He hit 40 or more home runs in four of the next five seasons. In fact, from 1955 to 1960, Ernie Banks hit more home runs (248) than Mickey Mantle. His biggest years were 1958 (47 home runs and 129 RBIs) and 1959 (45 home runs and 143 RBIs to lead the majors). Although Banks played for a second-division ballclub, he was named the NL Most Valuable Player both years.

Mr. Cub was once asked to explain where he hid the weight to produce his power at the plate. "I carry it in my toes," he said, smiling. "I have very muscular toes."

MEL OTT *511*

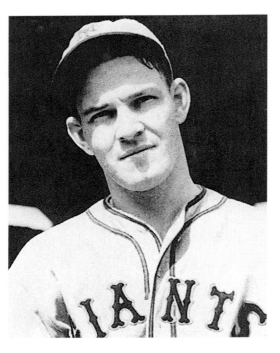

56

In 1925, at age sixteen, Mel Ott took a train from his home in Louisiana to see New York Giants manager John McGraw. The boy stood 5'9", weighed 170 pounds, and most of that weight was in his legs. He ran clumsily and at bat he lifted his thick right leg and strode before he swung. But he hit line drives off the short right-field wall in the Polo Grounds and McGraw got excited. "I don't give a damn about that crazy kick," he growled. "That kid's got one of the best natural swings I've ever seen."

(Left) Nineteen-year-old Mel Ott of the New York Giants.

At seventeen, Ott was a part-time Major Leaguer and in 1928, at nineteen, became the Giants' right fielder and batted .322. The next year, Master Melvin, as he was called, batted .328 and hit 42 home runs while driving in 151. Through twenty-plus seasons Ott was one of the most consistent hitters in the game. He batted over .300 eleven times. He scored over 100 runs nine times. He drove in over 100 runs nine times. And he was the hero of the Giants' defeat of the Washington Senators in the 1933 World Series, hitting for a .389 average and ripping two home runs.

"I don't give a damn about that crazy kick," said Giants manager John McGraw about Mel Ott. "That kid's got one of the best natural swings I've ever seen."

Ott was a big-leaguer at seventeen, a World Series star at twenty-four, manager of the Giants at thirty-three, a member of the Hall of Fame at forty-two and, sadly, dead at forty-nine, killed in a traffic accident. In between he kicked his leg and hit enough homers to gain entry into the exclusive 500 Club.

EDDIE MURRAY *504*

Unlike the other members of the 500 Club, Murray never hit more than 33 home runs in a single season. Only five times did he hit as many as 30 in a season. But the switch-hitting first baseman played twenty full seasons in the Major Leagues and was a model of consistency. He averaged 25 home runs for each of those seasons and finished with 504.

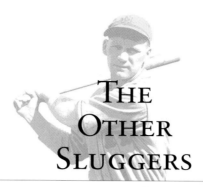

The Other Sluggers

Lee R. Schreiber

They dig in. They come hacking from their heels. They bop, bang, or clout like nobody's business. They are sweet swingers, big knockers, and long ballers. They are killers, hammers, and splinters. They are bambinos, sultans, and swatters.

They are the quintessential power hitters. We know about the sixteen members of the 500 Club; their feats have been detailed extensively in previous sections. But what about the other sluggers, power hitters who showed promise but never made it into the Club?

For any number of reasons, those other sluggers just didn't go the distance. Perhaps they simply lacked the right genes, technology, or geopolitical affiliations. Maybe it was just bad timing. Or worse luck. They, too, were professional hitters with wooden bats who, in any given year, time after time, went far and deep. But somehow, somewhere, they fell somewhat short.

JUST-SHORT BALL

Two names and their numbers stand out as prime examples of how the winds of fate propel some men to glory while denying (often equally deserving) others their due.

No catastrophic, or even particularly painful, end can explain why these two Hall of Famers fell so far short . . . just a nagging, aching back and oh, a world war.

Ralph Kiner ranks 47th in all-time taters with a total of 369 over a ten-year career. That's no small potatoes—more, say, than the 359 that Johnny Mize whipped up in fifteen seasons; or Yogi Berra's 358 in nineteen; or Boog Powell's 339 in seventeen. Kiner made the most of his decade, leading the league in roundtrippers a record seven straight years; driving in 100 or more runs six times; ranking first in slugging percentage three times; becoming the only person ever to

(Opposite) Ralph Kiner, here taking a cut at Pittsburgh Pirates spring training, was one of the most prolific home run hitters of his time, leading the National League in home runs for seven straight years, 1946–52.

61

62

(Left) The powerful swing of Hank Greenberg as seen from above.

homer in three consecutive All-Star Games (1949–51); and remaining third to Mark McGwire and Babe Ruth with a ratio of 7.1 home runs for every 100 at-bats. Had he been able to overcome a back sprain and finish another four seasons (at his annual 35-homer pace), Kiner would have overshot the magical 500 mark.

Hank Greenberg yanked out 331 roundtrippers in his thirteen big league years, though he exceeded 500 at-bats in only seven seasons. Moreover, after the attack on Pearl Harbor in 1941 (soon after winning his second MVP award), he swapped his Detroit jersey for a U.S. Army Air Corps uniform and did not return it until the summer of '45. The hometown celebration was completed when Greenberg's ninth-inning grand slam on the last day of the season clinched the pennant for the Tigers; yet, fans of the original Hammerin' Hank speculated about the numbers he could have posted in those four

(Opposite) Greenberg, of the Detroit Tigers, crossing the plate after hitting his third homer in a game against the St. Louis Browns in 1946. Greenberg led the American League that year with 44 homers.

potentially power-packed years. He was certainly not the only player to lose an irretrievable piece of his slugging life to military service—famously, Ted Williams missed part of two seasons during the Korean War—but Greenberg arguably seemed to have sacrificed the greatest (possible) numbers for his country. In the 5,193 at-bats he was allotted, he did manage to amass 379 doubles, 1,276 runs batted in (his RBI ratio of one per every 4.07 at bat ranks third all-time), and a home run ratio of 6.37 per 100 at-bats puts him within the top 15.

DEAD BALL

There were few truer power hitters in his day than "Wahoo" Sam Crawford. Unfortunately, his days were done before the polymer chemists got around to cooking up and filling baseballs with bountiful, bounciful cores of rubber. During this "dead ball" era, Crawford and his contact-minded cronies were content to hit it "where they ain't." In 1908, Wahoo set a record that will absolutely, 110-percent-positively never be broken: He led the league with a total of 7 four-baggers (a mark equaled by Red Murray in 1909 and Bob "Braggo" Roth in '15).

The deadliest force throughout much of this juiceless period was Frank "Home Run" Baker, who led the American League in jacks from 1911–14, with totals of 11, 10, 12, and 9, respectively (a mediocre month for McGwire).

The convergence of rubber and Ruth whacked this epoch back into the Stone Age. In 1920, after the Babe swatted an incredible 54 home runs, purists—and pitchers—raised complaints about the hopped-up "rabbit" balls (a disgruntled hurler said you could hold one up to your ear and "hear its little heart beating a mile a minute"). For most fans, however, this era was good and dead.

OH-SO-FOREIGN BALL

Many marginally talented ballplayers have reached, even passed, the 500 circuit-clout mark, yet will forever be diminished (and rightly so) for having done it with metallic softball bats or on soil foreign to North Americans. There was one man, however, who ultimately left some of the greatest names in baseball—Kadota (567), Nomura (657), Mays (660), Ruth (714), and Aaron (755)—choking on his domestic diamond dust.

64

Leading the American League with a whopping 11, 10, 12, and 9 homers from 1911–14, Frank "Home Run" Baker was considered a slugger supreme during the so-called "dead ball" era.

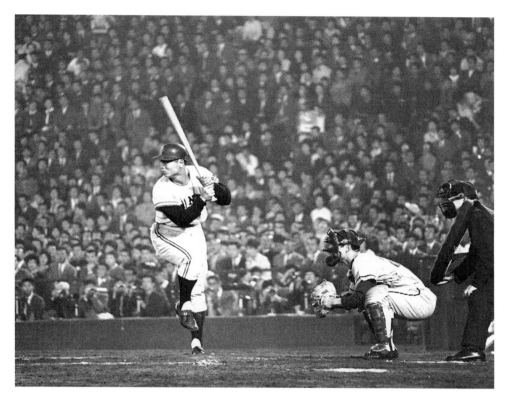

Sadaharu Oh, the man who hit more home runs (868) in his career than anyone else. In this 1964 photo, Oh displays his unusual hitting style of kicking out his leg before taking a swing.

Sadaharu Oh's 868 home runs over a twenty-three-year career (1958–80) surpasses anyone else in Japan, the United States, or any sovereign nation that boasts a professional baseball league. How, though, we can only wonder, would this son of a Chinese emigrant (his surname means "king" in both Chinese and Japanese) have fared against American pitching? "The opponents and I are really one," Oh has said of his native mound men. "My strength and skills are only half of the equation. The other half is theirs. An opponent is someone whose strength joined to yours creates a certain result."

A (AA & AAA) BALL

Crash Davis, the fictionalized Oh of the "bushies" played by Kevin Costner in *Bull Durham*, strongly and skillfully conjoined with minor league pitchers to capture the all-time (fictional) record of 246 knocks before promptly calling it a career. (In fact, he wouldn't have crashed into the top ten with such a meager minors collection.)

What about the real Crash Davis, some romantic character(s) awash in missed or lost opportunities who never quite made it in the Show? Who—and what—are the actual figures?

Start with numero uno, Hector Espino, and his 484 minor-league taters. Hector must have been partial to home cooking; other than 32 games for Jacksonville in 1964, he played all of his 24 pro baseball seasons in his native Mexican League (AAA equivalent). His top single-season home run total was 46.

Trailing Espino is Andres Mora, with 438, followed by spitball-pitcher-turned-outfielder Russell "Buzz" Arlett, who set off 432 bombs in the minors, but only 18 in his single big league season (with the Phillies in 1931). Nick Cullop cleaned 420 minor-league clocks, but stopped at 11 in his majors time. Merv Connors walloped an even 400 tonks in the minors but played exactly zero days in the bigs.

Sixth-ranked Joe Hauser (399), who knocked around Major League Baseball for parts of six seasons, may have been the greatest near-legend of them all. In 1923, his second year with the Athletics, "Unser Choe" ("Our Joe" in German) stopped the Show by finishing tied for fourth in home runs with Tris Speaker. In '24, the twenty-five-year-old first baseman's 27 clouts placed him second in the league to the Bambino. "Babe loved to pull my shirttail out every time he stopped at first base," Hauser said. "Lucky for me . . . he was usually on his way to another base." Unfortunately for our Joe, a broken leg ended his big league career, motivating

Joe Hauser, a minor-league long-ball legend.

him to make a name in the minors for perhaps the most storied four and a half seasons in any professional hacker's history. In 1930, he hit a record 63 homers for Baltimore; then led the league in '31 with 31; moved to Minneapolis the next season, where he topped the American Association with 49 round-trippers; re-set the record in '33 with 69 four-baggers; and began '34 on fire—with 33 HR and 88 RBI in only 82 games—before shattering his kneecap and, essentially, his career.

In 1954, Roswell's Joe Bauman set the professional single-season wooden-bat record of 72 homers in the Longhorn League; but, without a single lick in the majors, ultimately became just another in the long line of minor league phenoms who couldn't make the necessary adjustments...to bigger ballparks, better pitching, basic fundamentals.

66

THE ANTI-SLUGGER

Though this book is about the home run and a celebration of those who made it their business to hit home runs, we must not neglect the everyday ballplayers (pitchers excluded) who distinguished themselves by their distinct lack of power. These players may have excelled in other areas—speed, defense, even batting average—but they just were impotent when it came to the home run. Some examples of great anti-sluggers are Jerry Remy, who, in his last 2,292 at-bats with the Boston Red Sox before ending his career in 1984, went homerless, and Larry Bowa, the fine shortstop for the Philadelphia Phillies and Chicago Cubs, who in 8,418 career at-bats hit only 15 homers.

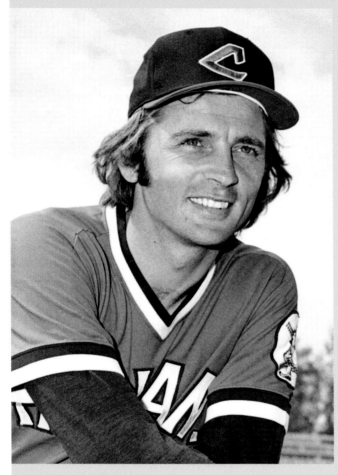

Duane Kuiper, who hit only one home run in his twelve-year career.

But the king of the anti-sluggers is Duane Kuiper. Kuiper played second base for the Cleveland Indians and was noted for his defensive skills, definitely not his slugging. Kuiper, in the 3,379 at-bats during his twelve-year career, hit just one home run for a home run hitting average, based on 600 at-bats a season, of .178, the lowest average for an everyday player.

Kuiper's one home run came off Steve Stone of the Chicago White Sox on August 29, 1977. After hitting the homer, Kuiper pondered his future as a home run hitter. "One is better than none," Kuiper said, "but any more than that and people start expecting them."

67

BLACK BALL

There are just so many adjustments a man can make. Josh Gibson, now acknowledged as one of the greatest ballplayers of the twentieth century, could not effect the single salient alteration—his color—that would have allowed him to suit up in the bigs. Instead, he tore up the Negro Leagues with other deserving stars like Cool Papa Bell, Satchel Paige, Pop Lloyd, Judy Johnson, Oscar Charleston, and Buck Leonard. A catcher blessed with first-rate defensive tools, Gibson generated most of his myth-making with the bat, compiling incredible stats and feats that may (or may not) have increased with the telling: nine home

Josh Gibson of the Homestead Grays of the Negro Leagues once hit 89 homers in a single season.

run titles; 89 dingers in a single season; .412 average in exhibitions against Major League pitching; several 600-foot shots and at least one that traveled 700 feet; 962 homers in all levels of competition over twenty-two years, despite playing most of his pro career in Forbes Field (a whopping 457 feet in center field—so deep that the batting cage was stored out there during games). Tragically, irrefutably, he died on January 20, 1947, a month after his thirty-fifth birthday (and three months before Jackie Robinson's Major League debut).

Other Negro Leaguers who could have done some permanent damage to big league home run records include George "Mule" Suttles, Willard "Home Run" Brown (nicknamed by Gibson for out-slugging him in their head-to-head confrontations), and even 5'7", 160-pound shortstop, Willie "the Devil" Wells ("the greatest money player in the game," said Cumberland Posey, owner of the Homestead Grays), who secured three Negro League home run titles and a career batting average of .334 before jumping to the Canadian Leagues.

A LEAGUE OF THEIR OWN

From 1943–54, great hitters such as Betty Jochum and Helen Callaghan had but one league in which to jump: the All-American Girls Professional Baseball League. For the first time, women had a competitive outlet in which to harness their ball-playing abilities. The level of play was high; but, much like the dead ball era, home run crowns barely cracked double digits. While both Jochum and Callaghan led the league in batting average, they each could only muster 7 career homers. It wasn't until the AAGPBL's last year of play that Babe-like Joanne Weaver finally struck the telling blows for genuine "girl power." Pound for pound, swing for swing, few pros of either stripe can lay claim to a finer batting line: In 93 games and 333 at-bats, she stroked 143 hits, scored 109 runs, stole 79 bases, and averaged .429; on the slugging side, she smacked 29 dingers and drove in 87 runs (while striking out only twenty-four times).

After the '54 season the league folded, leaving Weaver in the company of so many other worthy hackers who never quite fulfilled the promise of their early life's work.

They were professional hitters with wooden bats who, in any given year, time after time, could go deep. They knew how it was done, and how it often went. But they too soon learned how it goes . . . and is gone.

SINGLE-SEASON HOME RUN LEADERS

PLAYER	HR	TEAM	LEAGUE	YEAR
JOE BAUMAN	72	ROSWELL	LONGHORN	1954
MARK McGWIRE	70	ST. LOUIS	NATIONAL	1998
JOE HAUSER	69	MINNEAPOLIS	AM ASSN	1933
BOB CRUES	69	AMARILLO	W TEX-NM	1948
SAMMY SOSA	66	CHICAGO	NATIONAL	1998
MARK McGWIRE	65	ST. LOUIS	NATIONAL	1999
DICK STUART	66	LINCOLN	WESTERN	1956
BOB LENNON	64	NASHVILLE	SO ASSN	1954
SAMMY SOSA	63	CHICAGO	NATIONAL	1999
JOE HAUSER	63	BALTIMORE	INTL	1930
MOOSE CLABAUGH	62	TYLER	E TEX	1926
KEN GUETTLER	62	SHREVEPORT	TEXAS	1956
ROGER MARIS	61	NEW YORK	AMERICAN	1961
BABE RUTH	60	NEW YORK	AMERICAN	1927
TONY LAZZERI	60	SALT LAKE CITY	PACIFIC COAST	1925
FORREST KENNEDY	60	PLAINVIEW, TEX.	SOUTHWEST	1956

*North American Professional Leagues (MLB in CAPS)

70

(Above) Joe Bauman, of the Roswell
Rockets of the Longhorn League, jogs
home after hitting his 69th homer
of the 1954 season. Bauman ended
up with 72 for the year.

(Opposite page)
Sammy Sosa watches
his 61st homer leave the park
on September 13, 1998.

HOME RUNS HEARD 'ROUND THE WORLD

Ray Robinson

"Hartung down the line at third, not taking any chances. Lockman without too big of a lead at second, but he'll be running like the wind if Thomson hits one. Branca throws. There's a long drive. It's gonna be . . . I believe . . . The Giants win the pennant! The Giants win the pennant! The Giants win the pennant! Bobby Thomson hits into the lower deck of the left-field stands! The Giants win the pennant! And they're going crazy! They're going crazy! Oh-ho!"

—RUSS HODGES, NEW YORK GIANTS RADIO ANNOUNCER, OCTOBER 3, 1951

(Opposite) Bobby Thomson of the New York Giants striking the fatal blow to the Brooklyn Dodgers on October 3, 1951.

Baseball's lifeblood has long been an equal blend of conversation, memory, and statistics. Among the mega-stats the glamorous home run remains almighty and supreme, and the home run to win a game even more glamorous. Where then does that leave the home run to win a pennant or World Series in the rankings of glamour and drama? At the absolute top, of course.

Sometimes the mortals who delivered the deciding blows are made for the task, hitters known for their prodigious blasts. But then there are others whom we do not equate with the home run, unlikely heroes who, through odd circumstances and weird fate, along with one swing of their bat, became a part of baseball history and legend.

Perhaps the best example of one of those unlikely heroes is Bobby Thomson. Of the thousands of home runs bashed since the Babe departed from Brother Matthias's St. Mary's Industrial School for Boys in Baltimore, no single homer has held a more percussive impact than Thomson's "walk-off" blow at 3:58 P.M. on October 3, 1951. The setting was perfect for the soft-spoken New York Giant from Scotland and Staten Island. He came to the plate against the Brooklyn Dodgers' right-hander, Ralph Branca, in the last of the ninth inning of the decisive third game of the National League playoff. There were

74

two Giants on base, with the Dodgers ahead, 4–2. As Thomson left the Giants' dugout his combative manager, Leo Durocher, urged him to "hit one out." "But I was just thinking base hit, not homer," recalled Thomson, who had helped the Giants whittle away at the Dodgers' seemingly insurmountable mid-August lead of thirteen and a half games. "When I went to bat I kept calling myself all sorts of names—'get a hit, wait for the SOBs!' " Then Thomson's bat whirled around the second delivery from Branca (wearing the numeral 13 on his broad back) and the ball was on its mischievous journey—a low-flying drive into the lower-field stands of the Polo Grounds. Stunned left fielder Andy Pafko could only gaze up, in frustration, at the sphere.

Forever after millions would insist that they were present at this epiphanic moment. Thomson and Branca would be inextricably linked together, much like Alexander Hamilton and Aaron Burr, Jack Dempsey and Gene Tunney, William Jennings Bryan and Clarence Darrow. In truth, only thirty-four thousand were at the Polo Grounds

The trajectory of Thomson's shot and where it landed in the Polo Grounds.

to see it, some twenty thousand less than capacity. Other millions can tell you precisely where they were when Thomson swung for his "home run heard 'round the world." "The art of fiction is dead," wrote columnist Red Smith at the time. "Reality has strangled invention."

75

To this day Thomson's trophy ball has never been located, something of a subtheme of Don DeLillo's novel, *Underworld*. Only hours after the hit, the home run baseballs started to roll into Thomson. Many of those who were at the park claimed they had *the* ball, and would offer it to Bobby. Under such circumstances, it became clear that the actual ball would never be certified.

"I don't have the ball to this day," says Bobby, feeling slightly aggrieved. "If I did have it I'd always wonder whether that was really *the* ball."

A much less unlikely hero than Bobby Thomson was Ted Williams. Williams was a perennial All-Star who made hitting look so easy it appeared almost mundane. But Williams also had an uncanny knack for the dramatic best exemplified in three separate episodes. In the All-Star Game of 1941, at Detroit, in the bottom of the ninth inning, with two men on base, Ted crushed a pitch from the National League's Claude Passeau, to win the game for the American League, 7–5. It was the year Williams hit over .400 but he may have gotten

Thomson is mauled by his teammates, fans, and even manager (that's Leo Durocher, hatless and hairless, trying to get a piece of his home run hero), as he has just won the pennant for the New York Giants with his ninth-inning, three-run homer.

more sheer joy out of that blow than he did out of his swollen average. "Boy, wasn't that a pip!" he exclaimed in the clubhouse after the game, like a boy who had just crashed an old sock of a ball into a schoolhouse window.

In 1946, playing in his backyard at Fenway Park, Ted again put the icing on the American League's All-Star Game victory, with a truly amazing homer against Rip Sewell's infamous "eephus pitch." Sewell had come up with a pitch thrown so high—and slow— that a trailer truck could have been driven under it. Hitters were insulted by such "junk," which caused them to whale away in such futility at Sewell's

The home run swing of Ted Williams.

76

exaggerated motion. But this time Ted was primed for the challenge. As the ball descended from its ridiculous arc, Williams took two steps forward to meet it. The ball landed in the Red Sox right-field bull pen beyond the 380-foot mark. Even Sewell had to appreciate Ted's artistry, for as Ted ran out his home run the pitcher jogged alongside him, fairly screaming his congratulations at the kid.

Williams's final big league homer in his last game at Fenway Park in September of 1960 was also something to behold, even if only ten thousand die-hard Red Sox fans were there. At the age of forty-two, Ted was at the end of a career of triumphs, tumult, sulks, and wars (two) and he seemed to have barely enough strength to play three innings without puffing hard. But in the eighth inning he rose to the occasion once more and belted his 521st homer against Jack Fisher of Baltimore.

Employing his classic swing—long, smooth, and quick—Williams spelled finish to his playing life. "He ran, as he always ran out his homers, hurriedly, unsmiling, head down, as if praise were a storm of rain to get out of the way of," wrote John Updike.

In the locker room Ted was exultant but unyielding. "I really wanted that one," he said. "When I hit it I was hoping it would go." But then he added he had never had any intention of tipping his cap,

a gesture he had always denied his imploring fans. "Now it is done," he said.

Another Red Sox icon, not precisely in the Williams mold, was Carlton Fisk, a sturdy defensive catcher. In the twelfth inning of the sixth game of the 1975 World Series between Boston and Cincinnati's Big Red Machine, Fisk proved that God was not always scheming against the Red Sox. Many have rated this 241-minute game at Fenway Park as the greatest baseball contest ever played. It was a game full of rallies, counter-rallies, cartoon character heroes, comebacks, glorious catches, a record twelve pitchers, and the pièce de résistance, the climactic home run by Fisk. Others also credit this game with providing baseball with sufficient oxygen to face the upcoming years of free agency turmoil and endless salary squabbles.

A knee injury almost wrecked Fisk's career in 1974. The next year he broke his arm in the first game of the exhibition season. By June, however, he was back and hitting over .300. When Fisk came to bat in the sixth game of the World Series against the Reds, the score was tied at 6–6. A notorious right-handed pull-hitter, Fisk had confronted Fenway's Green Monster in left field many times. On Pat Darcy's first pitch, Fisk swung mightily (and now mythically) and the ball soared into the darkness of the night. As millions held their collective breaths in front of TV sets, Fisk took a step forward, then stopped and watched, urging the ball's flight until at last it bounced off the mesh attached to the left-field foul pole, some 304 feet away. Raising his fists above his head and leaping into the air like a crazed gazelle, Fisk made his way around the bases with the game-winner. His teammates mobbed him as church bells pealed throughout Massachusetts.

78

Normally a taciturn man, Fisk described his reaction to the moment. "It seemed like the wait for Christmas morning," he said. He would always acknowledge that that October night in Boston was the highlight of his baseball life. For baseball fans everywhere, even those who did not necessarily root for the Red Sox, it was a classic landmark of a game, with square-jawed Fisk playing the central role.

If Boston's fans thrilled to Fisk's exploit, they were chilled to the marrow by Bucky Dent's unexpected home run in the American League division playoff of 1978 between the Yankees and the Red Sox. That year, Dent, out of Georgia, was a light-hitting shortstop known for his solid defense, and spear-carrier on a Yankee team that boasted such marquee players as Reggie Jackson, Graig Nettles, Thurman Munson, Chris Chambliss, Ron Guidry, and Goose Gossage. In 1978 Dent batted just .243. Yet, in the seventh inning of the one-game battle in Fenway Park for supremacy of the American League East division, it was Dent, with only four home runs up to that point in 377 at-bats, who hit a home run into the 23-foot net above the Green Monster. There were two Yankees on base, with the New Yorkers behind 2–0. But with a soft breeze blowing toward left field, Dent's borrowed bat connected on a two-strike delivery from pitcher Mike Torrez, plunging New Englanders into Stygian gloom. The game and the pennant were lost; the Curse of the Bambino persisted. As Dent's "bloop" or "lucky poke" was written into baseball's history,

Game 6 of the 1975 World Series. (Opposite left) With the game tied in the twelfth inning, Carlton Fisk of the Boston Red Sox swings at Cincinnati's Pat Darcy's first pitch. (Opposite right) Fisk urges the ball to stay fair. (Left) And it does! Let the celebrations begin.

79

Boston manager Don Zimmer rancorously changed Bucky's name to "Bucky F——g Dent." As far as Dent is concerned, he is willing to let Zimmer call him anything he wants.

When it comes to serendipitous homers, Bill Mazeroski can challenge Bucky Dent any day. In the tumultuous World Series of 1960 between Pittsburgh and the Yankees (the Yankees outscored the Pirates 55–27, yet lost the series in seven games), the twenty-four-

year-old Mazeroski was the Yankee-slayer. Normally celebrated for his excellent coverage of second base, Mazeroski suddenly emerged in the last inning of the Series as Pittsburgh's Lochinvar. Ralph Terry, a right-hander, released the pitch to Mazeroski and the ball screeched off Maz's bat high over the left-field wall of Forbes Field. Yogi Berra, in left field that afternoon, could do little more than watch forlornly as the ball disappeared. Was there a bit of déjà vu here, with 1951's Andy Pafko?

The blow settled the issue at 10–9 for the Pirates, as the hometown fans went berserk. Mazeroski leapfrogged around the bases, an Everyman who had become the first player ever to end a World Series with an electrifying shot into the stands. Mazeroski could have been elected Pittsburgh's mayor on the spot. "I can't even talk. I'm too tired," he said breathlessly after the game that gave Pittsburgh its first World Series triumph in thirty-five years. Each year since Mazeroski's home run a group of admirers has gathered at the site of the blow to honor their hero. So far Mazeroski, a shy man, hasn't accepted an invitation to join them; it is not his style.

Cursed again? Unlikely hero Bucky Dent of the New York Yankees sends Boston's Mike Torrez's pitch over Fenway's Green Monster for a three-run homer that Red Sox (and Yankee) fans will never forget.

"We have a big 3–2 pitch coming from Eckersley. Gibson swings and a fly ball to deep right. This is gonna be a home run! Unbelievable! A home run for Gibson and the Dodgers have won, 5–4. I don't believe what I just saw! I don't believe what I just saw!"

—JACK BUCK, RADIO ANNOUNCER FOR GAME ONE OF THE 1988 WORLD SERIES.

Unlike Mazeroski and Dent, Kirk Gibson of the Los Angeles Dodgers was known as a power hitter. A former All-American football player at Michigan State, he could have been awarded honors, with his disheveled, thinning hair, and two-day stubble, for unkemptness. But he was also an athlete with pride and guts. Before the World Series of 1988 between the Dodgers and Oakland he was tormented by a torn hamstring and a sprained knee. His manager, Tommy Lasorda, hadn't expected to use him in the postseason and Gibson wasn't going to suit up.

But in the bottom of the ninth inning of the first game, with Oakland ahead 4–3, Mike Davis got on for the Dodgers with two out. Despite his physical condition, Gibson had prepared himself for such an emergency call. "I practiced in the clubhouse, hitting a ball off a tee," Gibson recalled. "Each swing caused me pain and agony. But I told Tommy I had one good swing in me."

An ecstatic Bill Mazeroski is jubilantly escorted to a mobbed home plate after shocking the New York Yankees with a ninth-inning home run to win the 1960 World Series for the Pittsburgh Pirates.

81

So Lasorda called on his stricken slugger, who limped to the plate as the crowd in Dodger Stadium roared its support. They were voting for effort, since many of them probably didn't think he could deliver. Gibson proceeded to foul four straight pitches off the relief ace, Dennis Eckersley, each time wincing. On the next pitch, a slider, Gibson sent a long home run into space to win the game. As he trotted gimpily around the bases, Gibson expressed his joy by pumping his arms vigorously. It was the only time he would bat in the Series— and the Dodgers would win it, due in no small measure to Gibson's transcendent moment. Had he been a little blonder, Gibson would have been a carbon copy of Robert Redford in *The Natural*.

After his "one good swing" off Oakland relief ace Dennis Eckersley wins game one of the 1988 World Series, Kirk Gibson of the Los Angeles Dodgers celebrates as he limps around the bases.

A MOST DUBIOUS HOME RUN

There is evidence of numerous home runs that were mistakenly ruled foul balls or ground rule doubles, but the instances of the opposite, home runs granted that were, in reality, not home runs at all are few, and records kept of them are yet to be unearthed. There is one, however, that will live in infamy.

It was game one of the 1996 American League Championship Series between the New York Yankees and Baltimore Orioles at Yankee Stadium. In the eighth inning, with the Yankees trailing 4–3, the Yankee rookie shortstop, Derek Jeter, came to the plate. The right-handed-hitting Jeter drove a pitch by Arthur Rhodes toward the right-field stands. The Orioles rightfielder, Tony Tarasco, went back to the wall, waited for the ball to settle in his glove, when, out of nowhere, a hand reached over the railing and snatched the ball before Tarasco could catch it.

Tony Tarasco of the Baltimore Orioles stretches for Derek Jeter's ball, but it's twelve-year-old fan Jeffrey Maier (with glove) who makes the catch.

Rich Garcia, the right field umpire, immediately signaled home run despite Tarasco's pointing emphatically to the fan who robbed him of the catch. Garcia ruled that the fan did not interfere with the ball, but from the television replay, it appeared the fan reached over the rail to catch the ball. The "home run" tied the game, and the Yankees eventually went on to win 5–4 and then defeat the Orioles in the Series in five games.

The fan was twelve-year-old Jeffrey Maier, and he immediately went on to become a local and even national celebrity. Though his fame didn't last much longer than the allotted fifteen minutes, it was long enough for Maier to be invited to a banquet where Derek Jeter was also in attendance. When asked if he talked to young Jeffrey, Jeter replied that he had. What was it he said to the boy?

"Thank you," Jeter said.

83

Few would argue against the proposition that the most virtuoso home run performance of all time was delivered by Reggie Jackson of the Yankees in the 1977 World Series against the Los Angeles Dodgers. As the self-confessed "straw that stirs the drink," Reggie stirred as no slugger before him in the sixth game at Yankee Stadium, as fifty-six thousand looked on in awe.

In the fourth inning Reggie hit the first pitch from Burt Hooton into the right-field seats, putting the Yanks ahead 4–3. In the fifth inning, with a man on base, Reggie again hit the first pitch, this one delivered by Elias Sosa, into the Ruthville section of the stadium, to give the Yanks a 7–3 lead. Then, coming up as the lead-off batter in the eighth, Reggie zeroed in on another Dodger pitcher, Charlie

84

Hough, and sent his slow motion knuckle ball over 450 feet into dead center field, an area unoccupied by fans.

The Babe had hit three homers in a Series game twice, in 1926 and 1928—but never three in a row and never on consecutive pitches. "When Reggie hit the third one," Steve Garvey, the Dodgers' first baseman, admitted later, "I applauded in my glove." With an ego even lustier than his swing, Jackson had become New York's man of the hour. Would any mortal ever equal or surpass such a feat? Unlikely. Just ask Reggie Jackson.

It would seem that nothing could match the pressure of coming up in a big spot during a playoff or World Series game and trying to deliver the decisive blow. But Mark McGwire, during the last week-

Reggie Jackson's three home run swings in game 6 of the 1977 World Series shown in order, left to right.

end of the 1998 season, his St. Louis Cardinals long out of playoff contention, was also confronted with unseemly pressure. The pressure, in this case, was applied by the irrepressible Sammy Sosa of the Chicago Cubs. Mark's booster rocket race with Sosa, with the media examining every particle of his private life and his being, left him frazzled. "He was like a downed power line in a storm," wrote Tom Verducci of *Sports Illustrated*.

Going into the last Friday of the 1998 season, McGwire, built like a Percheron and seemingly as powerful, didn't even boast the largest total of home runs in the National League. Sosa was ahead of him, 66–65. With seventy-two hours to go it appeared that 70 was out of reach for McGwire, as he went into a final series with Montreal on

On the last day of the 1998 season, Mark McGwire connects on his 70th home run.

his home turf. He couldn't wait to be released from his burden, even as his competitive juices flowed from within him.

Then, in what must be regarded as one of the most remarkable feats of home run hitting in history, Big Mac exploded for five home runs in the next three days. Homer-happy Americans applauded him—and so did his generous, friendly rival, Sosa.

First, McGwire connected against right-hander Shayne Bennett. Then, in the next eighteen swings of his bat he produced four more titanic blasts, to reach 70. Dusty Hermanson threw the 67th homer, Kirk Bullinger threw 68, Mike Thurman the 69th, and, finally, on Sunday, in the seventh inning, with two runners on base, two out, and the scored tied, McGwire unloaded one last time for the year on Carl Pavano.

McGwire had been walked intentionally with first base open in the fifth inning. But in McGwire's next time at bat Pavano made up his mind to "go right after" Mark. Not to be denied, McGwire went right after Pavano, turning Pavano's 96-mile-an-hour fastball into his magic 70th home run. As the fans roared in disbelief, McGwire circled the bases for the last time in 1998.

Throughout the year McGwire had remained understated and every bit a mensch. After number 70, he remained in character. "I think the magnitude of the number won't be understood for quite a while," he said, in his assessment. "It's really unheard of for someone to hit 70 home runs. So, I'm like in awe of myself right now."

The 70th home run baseball, already firmly entrenched in baseball's mythology, cost a collector three million dollars, the largest sum ever doled out for a single baseball artifact.

How much will be paid for number 75—or even number 80, if it ever comes to that? Or for other home runs heard 'round the world?

HOME RUNS HEARD ALMOST 'ROUND THE WORLD

T hose who might object to some of our climactic home run choices might take solace in a couple of attractive alternates. Although he was not one of the more glamorous Yankee home run bashers, Chris Chambliss accounted for one of the team's most famous home runs. On October 14, 1976, Chambliss's blast in

the ninth inning of game five of the Yankee–Kansas City American League playoff broke a 6–6 tie and won the flag for the New Yorkers. A pennant famine of twelve years was thus brought to an end.

In 1993, Joe Carter of the Toronto Blue Jays, a muscular outfielder, ended the World Series against the Phillies with a two-out, three-run home run off Mitch Williams in game six. It marked only the second time in Series history that the classic had closed out with a four-baser.

(Above) Chris Chambliss fruitlessly tries to find home plate after hitting the home run that won the 1976 American League pennant for the Yankees and returned them to the World Series after a twelve-year drought.

(Right) Joe Carter leaps in joy as his three-run homer wins the 1993 World Series for the Toronto Blue Jays.

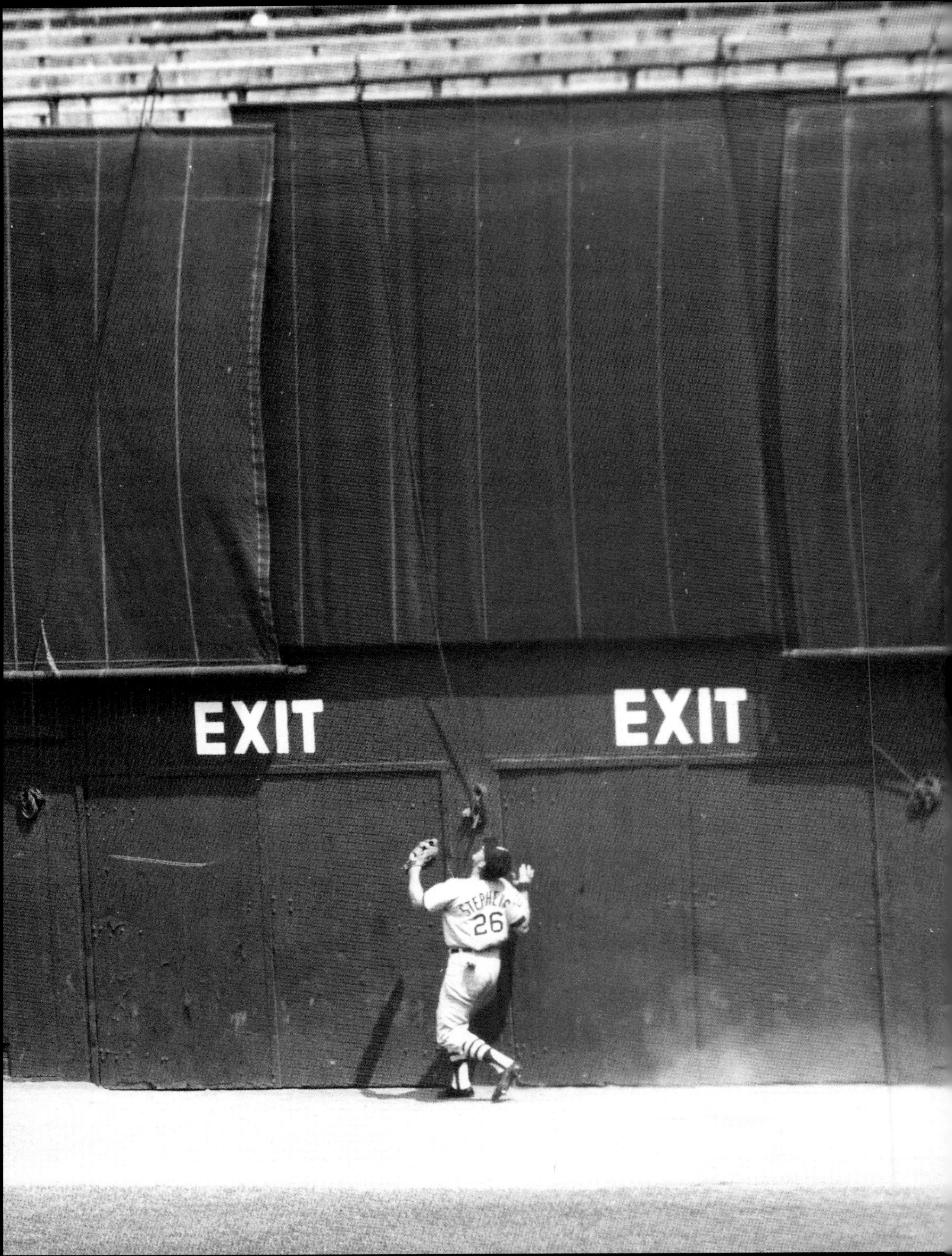
EXIT
EXIT
STEPHENSON
26

MONUMENTAL BLASTS

Brian Silverman

(Opposite) In a game in 1964, Gene Stephens of the Chicago White Sox watches a ball hit by Mickey Mantle sail over a screen put up to black out the center-field bleachers in the old Yankee Stadium. The ball (seen at the top of the photo) cleared the screen above the 461-foot mark and, at the time, was believed to be the longest ball hit to that part of the stadium.

On September 8, 1998, in front of a capacity crowd at Busch Stadium in St. Louis and millions of television viewers worldwide, Mark McGwire hit his sixty-second home run of the season, a line shot over the left field wall. As McGwire took his celebratory trot around the bases, accepting congratulations from Cub players and Cardinal coaches along the way for shattering Roger Maris's single-season home run record, and before he could even hug his son, Matt, at home plate, the distance of that historic home run had been posted on the Busch Stadium scoreboard: a measly 341 feet. In a year of titanic blasts, it was McGwire's shortest homer of the year. But, like the preceding 61 and the eight that followed in his record-setting, 70 home run season, the distances of all his home runs had been measured and displayed.

It's a relatively new phenomenon, this instant electronic verification of home run distances. But it is one that now is as much a part of baseball stadium procedure as the posting of out-of-town scores. We want to know, and immediately, how far a home run travels. And we want those figures to be as accurate as possible because we have the technology to make them so. We have instant replay and computer grids formatted to the parameters and configurations of each ballpark that measure the parabolic trajectory of home run flight paths. Our eyes and memory, it seems, when it comes to accurately judging home run distances, have become obsolete.

But thankfully, it was eyes and memory that documented the mammoth home runs of the past. There were no computer grids, no instant replay; only the tales of eyewitnesses. And, over time, as the eyes weaken and the memory fades, those tales somehow seem to get taller and taller.

There is no shortage of tale tellers of the feats of Babe Ruth and the tales, like Ruth himself, are often larger than life. The same can be said about many of his home runs, some of them rumored to have traveled anywhere from 500 to 1,000 feet.

The first taste of Ruth's massive power came on July 21, 1915, when, as a rookie pitcher with the Boston Red Sox, he clouted a pitch in Sportsman's Park in St. Louis that carried over the right-field bleachers and landed on a sidewalk across Grand Boulevard, approximately 470 feet from home plate. No one was supposed to hit a ball that far...especially not a pitcher.

As a pitcher, Ruth's power was wasted, so he was converted to an everyday player. History has proven that a very wise move. And in 1921, it is believed that Ruth hit at least one 500-foot home run in all eight American League cities. But, with all his World Series appearances, Ruth tortured ballparks in both leagues, and a few, in particular, stand out. On June 8, 1926, in Detroit, Ruth blasted a homer to right-center field that was reported to have traveled more than 600 feet. The ball cleared the wall, bounced off the top of a parked car, and rolled to a stop two blocks away. A baseball writer named H. G.

Babe Ruth was a larger-than-life character, as were many of the monstrous home runs he hit.

Salsinger claimed the ball traveled 602 feet in the air and stopped rolling 800 to 850 feet from home plate. He had fans sign an affidavit to his claim, but he never paced off the distance, so, despite the affidavits, his account was disregarded.

Before the upper deck in old Comiskey Park was built, Ruth, in 1927, apparently cleared the right-field stands. The eyewitness in this case was Bill Downes, a batboy for the White Sox, who recalled the blast: "It was a line shot that kept rising. After clearing the park, it landed in a soccer field behind the right-field stands and kept rolling until it came to a rest near the old Armory on what was then Wentworth Avenue." According to calculations, that would make 800 feet away from home plate.

One thing most of the sluggers of tape-measure home runs have in common is size. These are big men. Men with abundant girth. Men with many muscles. And one of the most muscular was Jimmie Foxx. Foxx, who played for the Philadelphia Athletics and Boston Red Sox, was a rock solid 6 feet, 195 lbs. "He has muscles in his hair," commented Lefty Gomez, a pitcher for the New York Yankees who was often tormented by Foxx's immense power.

91

Jimmie Foxx, who pitcher Lefty Gomez said was so strong he had "muscles in his hair," is seen here in 1942 getting assistance in putting on his new Chicago Cubs uniform from his son, Jimmie Jr.

Gomez once claimed that Foxx hit the longest home run in Yankee Stadium . . . off him. The homer, according to Gomez's account, landed in the left-field grandstand in the old stadium. And it was hit with such force that it broke the back of a seat near the last row. "When Neil Armstrong first set foot on the moon, he and all the space scientists were puzzled by an unidentifiable white object. I knew immediately what it was. That was a home run ball hit off me in 1937 by Jimmie Foxx," Gomez reminisced years later.

"Foxx hit the ball so far so often that we didn't pay much attention to most of them," said Bill Werber, a teammate of Foxx's on the Red Sox. One homer Werber and many others did pay attention to occurred at Comiskey Park in Chicago in 1936. Foxx delivered a drive that cleared the roof, the street, a parking lot, and a tennis court. No one bothered to pace the distance, but a peanut vendor under the stands said he heard it "clear as a shot." And who are we to doubt a peanut vendor?

Ruth hit his long home runs left-handed, Foxx hammered his from the right side, but no one had done it from both sides of the plate until a muscle-chiseled nineteen-year-old kid from Oklahoma arrived in the big city of New York. The kid was Mickey Mantle and his incredible power first became apparent in his rookie season with the New York Yankees in 1951. On a barnstorming trip on the west coast during spring training, the Yankees were playing the University of Southern California Trojans in an exhibition game. In the game, a 15–1 rout by the Yankees, Mantle hit two homers—one left-handed, the other from the right side—a triple, and a single, and drove in seven runs. But it was the homer hit left-handed that had everyone talking. "It was like a golf ball going into orbit. It was hit so far it was like it wasn't real," said Rod Dedeaux, the coach of USC said. Gil McDougald, who played with Mantle for ten years, reflected years later that it was the longest ball he ever saw the Mick hit.

Mickey Mantle could hit home runs long distances from both sides of the plate.

The ball flew over the 439 mark in centerfield and just kept flying, passing over the 160-foot width of a football field until it finally hit a fence on one hop. The estimated distance of the blow was 660 feet. "It was a superhuman feat," Dedeaux added. And it made the 500-plus-foot homer he hit right-handed that day seem minuscule in comparison.

Bring on the Tape Measure

Something had to be done. Those unscientific estimations of the distances of Mantle's home runs were a mockery. Those hearsay accounts of his momentous drives were exaggerated. Fact had to be separated from fiction. So on April 17, 1953, in Griffith Stadium in Washington, the New York Yankee publicist, Red Patterson, was ready. The pitcher for the Senators was Chuck Stobbs. Mantle, batting right-handed, launched a rocket that nicked, but cleared, the 60-foot-high scoreboard in left-center at the 391 marker, and exited the stadium, landing, eventually, in the backyard of a house on the other side of a three-story building that bordered the stadium.

Knowing he had witnessed something very special, Patterson immediately left the press box to search for the ball. "I saw a kid running down the street with a ball and asked him where he had gotten it. He showed me the yard and I paced off the distance back to where it was already measured on the outfield fence," said Patterson. The distance he came up with was 565 feet. The Tape-Measure Home Run was born.

Yankee Stadium, where Mickey Mantle played half of his games, was a big ballpark. There had been many home runs hit there, but no one had ever displayed the awesome power needed to hit one completely out of the Stadium. Mantle, on May 22, 1963, in a game

The diagram of the path of the home run hit by Mickey Mantle on May 22, 1963 that just missed exiting Yankee Stadium.

against Kansas City, came awfully close. Bill Fischer, the Kansas City pitcher, delivered, and Mantle, batting left-handed, rocketed the ball off the facade of the right-field roof, 115 feet high and 367 feet away. "It was like a plane taking off," said longtime Yankee announcer Mel Allen. "The *New York Times* saw fit to diagram, by triangulation, the ball from home plate. They said if it hadn't hit the triple-tiered facade, the ball might have reached the Bronx County Courthouse two blocks up the street."

Estimated at 620 feet, Mantle called it the hardest ball he ever hit, but, in his usual self-effacing manner, declared rival slugger, Frank

94

Frank Howard, whom Mickey Mantle called "the strongest man I ever saw."

Howard, the man who hit the hardest, and longest, home runs he had ever seen. "He was the strongest I ever saw," Mantle once said of Howard. "I saw him hit a line drive off Whitey Ford at the stadium [Yankee Stadium] that Whitey actually jumped for, it was hit that low. It ended up hitting the speakers behind the monuments in dead center [for a home run]."

The 6'7", 275-pound Howard played in both the American and National Leagues and his home runs were as gargantuan as his physique. But Howard never considered himself a distance home run hitter. "More of my home runs were line drives," he has said. "The only satisfaction in hitting it a hundred or a hundred and fifty feet longer than usual was knowing I had everything together . . . bat speed, balance, leverage."

Howard had everything together when, playing for the Los Angeles Dodgers in the 1963 World Series against the Yankees, he hit another shot off Whitey Ford that landed in the loge seats at Dodger Stadium. "I know that one went over five hundred feet, but it wasn't my longest," Howard said.

The longest home run Howard claims to have hit happened at Forbes Field in Pittsburgh. The moon shot struck a light tower high above the 407-foot mark in left center. Howard estimated the homer to have traveled 600 feet. Despite his claims to the contrary, anyone who could torch the upper deck of Washington's Robert F. Kennedy Stadium as many times as he did (24) is most certainly a long-ball, tape-measure slugger.

While Howard was bombarding Robert F. Kennedy Stadium, not too far up the turnpike, Dick (also known as Richie) Allen of the Philadelphia Phillies was blasting balls to infinite distances at Connie Mack Stadium. Allen, using a massive 42-ounce bat, sent 18 home

Pittsburgh's Forbes Field and the light tower in left centerfield that Frank Howard hit with one of his massive home runs.

Dick Allen, seen here as a rookie for the Philadelphia Phillies in 1964, and the 42-ounce bat that he used in whacking 18 home runs over the grandstand at Connie Mack Stadium in Philadelphia.

96   runs over the 75-foot-high left-field grandstand at Connie Mack Stadium. Of those 18, two are particularly memorable. On May 29, 1965, against the Chicago Cubs, Allen tattooed a Larry Jackson pitch, sending the ball over an advertising billboard on top of the left-centerfield roof, 529 feet from home plate. Two years later, on July 9, Allen smoked a pitch from Nelson Briles of the St. Louis Cardinals that cleared the center-field wall between the flagpole and the upper deck, the only time a ball ever left the park at that spot.

Despite his awesome power, the enigmatic Dick Allen was often booed by the hometown fans. Pittsburgh Pirate slugger Willie Stargell had a theory about that. "He never hit those people a souvenir. He hit 'em all over the roof and out of the park," Stargell said. "That's why those people in Philadelphia booed Richie so much."

Willie "Pops" Stargell was one to talk about hitting balls out of parks. In his twenty-one-year career as a Pittsburgh Pirate, Stargell hit seven home runs over the 90-foot-high right-field roof at Forbes Field and twice cleared Dodger Stadium, once in 1969 and again in 1973.

Though he played in Pittsburgh, Pops treated Montreal like a second home when it came to hitting tape-measure homers. At old Jarry Park, the original home of the Expos, Stargell hit a shot that landed in a swimming pool 200 feet beyond the right-field fence.

(Left) Willie Stargell of the Pittsburgh Pirates, here connecting on a home run in the 1979 National League Championship Series against the Cincinnati Reds, hit seven home runs over the right-field roof at Forbes Field.

Later, after the Expos moved into Olympic Stadium, he delivered another into the second deck of right field. Estimated at 535 feet, the homer is considered the longest ever hit at Olympic Stadium. To commemorate the legendary blast, there is a gold star on the seat where the ball struck. "I didn't hit 'em to show anybody up, but I didn't apologize for how far I hit 'em," Stargell said.

Reggie Jackson never apologized for the long home runs he hit, either. In fact, he usually spent a few moments savoring them from home plate. "I've gotten pitchers angry by putting on a floor show," Jackson said. "But I love to hit that little round ball and make them say 'Wow!'"

Jackson had them saying "wow" during the 1971 All-Star Game in Detroit. In the game, Jackson rocketed a Dock Ellis pitch off a power transformer above the Tiger Stadium roof in right center. Had it not hit the

(Below) Olympic Stadium in Montreal, where there is a gold star on a seat in the second deck above right field to commemorate the longest homer ever hit there, struck by the powerful Willie Stargell in 1978.

98

transformer, estimates were that the ball would have traveled more than 600 feet. Al Kaline, the former Detroit Tiger and a Hall of Famer, called it the hardest hit ball he had ever seen. From a man who said he would rather hit than have sex, we can only just imagine the sensation Reggie Jackson felt as he was slowly circling the bases after that shot.

Unlike Reggie, we rarely knew what slugger Dave Kingman felt because he was a man of very few words. But if his bat could talk, the tales it would tell would be of wondrous power. The well-traveled Kingman played for, among others, the Cubs, Mets, Yankees, and Athletics. Standing 6'6" and weighing 210 pounds, Kingman was never cheated on a swing. Oftentimes he flapped at air, but when Kingman did connect, the ball could travel unheard of distances. In an exhibition game against the Yankees in the mid-1970s, Kingman hit a ball off Catfish Hunter that Hunter himself calculated at 1,200 feet. "Six hundred feet up," Hunter said, "and six hundred feet out."

Reggie Jackson, here taking a big swing, hit one of the longest home runs in All-Star Game history in Detroit in 1971.

Another moon shot credited to Kingman happened on April 14, 1976 when "Kong," as he was affectionately called by his fans, sent a ball out of Wrigley Field in Chicago and over Waveland Avenue, eventually smacking against an apartment house. The estimate of Kingman's Chicago shot is 630 feet, but purists would like to put an asterisk next to it. After all, the wind was blowing out that day in Chicago. Baseball purists can be very fickle. A wind-aided home run, albeit one that was estimated at 630 feet, in their minds, just doesn't measure up.

(Left) Dave Kingman in a Mets uniform in 1981. When he connected, the ball could travel unheard-of distances.

But to satisfy those purists, most Major League clubs, beginning in 1982, adopted a computerized system developed by IBM to measure home runs as accurately as possible. Balls were flying out of parks at alarming rates and amazing distances. There were the ongoing outcries that the ball had been livened up. It was an allegation that had gone on for years and one that Mickey Mantle, when he was playing, responded to by saying that maybe it wasn't the ball, that "maybe it was the players who were livelier."

The players may or may not be livelier, but one thing is certain: They are bigger and stronger than ever. Take the 6'4", 240-pound José Canseco for example. When Canseco takes a swing, all of his bulging muscles are in motion, and the ball, if he connects solidly, usually travels staggeringly long distances. After Canseco hit the second of two home runs in a game in Oakland in 1990, the victimized pitcher, Paul Mirabella, said, "I wasn't worried about the ball going out of the park. I was just wondering if it was going to land in San Francisco. [The homer] had a crew of four and a meal."

(Above) José Canseco and his bulging muscles.

100

Mark McGwire, as a member of the Oakland Athletics, hitting another of his titanic homers.

Canseco's best known stratospheric shot came in game four of the 1989 American League Championship Series in the Skydome in Toronto. The home run traveled to the far reaches of the fifth deck of the Sky Dome and was estimated, by computer grid, at 484 feet.

It didn't help Paul Mirabella or any other pitcher at the time that Canseco's teammate on the Oakland Athletics was another behemoth named Mark McGwire. The 6'5", 250-pound McGwire would, seemingly, be more suited to defensive end than first baseman, and, though his bulk stretches the confines of a baseball uniform, it fits him better than shoulder pads and a football helmet ever would. Looking back now, after all he has accomplished, it's hard to believe that, when the two played together in Oakland, McGwire's home runs were actually overshadowed by Canseco's. Sure, he was a feared hitter and recorded some momentous blasts, but it really wasn't until the second half of the decade of the 1990s that Big Mac emerged as the home run titan in both quantity and quality.

The quantity—his 52 home runs in 1996, the 58 in 1997, the historic 70 in 1998, and his 65 in 1999—we all know about. A bit lost in the numbers are the size of McGwire's homers. Let's start with a game in Seattle in 1997. McGwire, still with the Oakland Athletics, was facing the Mariners' ace, Randy Johnson. It was a classic confrontation: power versus power. Johnson delivered a pitch that radar estimated at 97 mph. McGwire connected and that same radar caught the pitch leaving McGwire's bat at 105 mph. At that speed it didn't take long for the ball to land eleven rows up in section 242, high into the Kingdome's upper deck. About forty seconds after the blast, using a calculation from a computer grid, the length of the homer was estimated at 538 feet. "He's not human," Canseco said of McGwire. "Mac's an alien from the future who has come back to show us how to play this game."

Most of the 70 home runs Mark McGwire hit in 1998 were monumental blasts, but this one, his 62nd, traveled just 341 feet.

"Someday when I have children, I'll tell them about it," said Mark Bellhorn of the A's, an eyewitness to the mammoth homer.

There would be more to tell the children from the legend of Mark McGwire. The next year, 1998, as a member of the St. Louis Cardinals and during the record-setting 70 home run season, McGwire surpassed the 500-foot mark in distance of home run ten times, but the longest occurred on May 16 at Busch Stadium. The pitcher was Livan Hernandez of the Florida Marlins. McGwire was leading off in the bottom of the fourth when he launched a Hernandez pitch

101

deep toward center field. "I think I saw it hit a sign in center field and drop down to the field, but I wasn't sure," said John Vuch, manager of baseball information and assistant for player development for the Cardinals—and the man responsible for measuring home runs hit at Busch Stadium. "In my twenty years with the Cardinals, I've never seen a ball hit that far. Balls just don't go there. I doubted my eyes."

Usually Vuch estimates the distances of the home runs at Busch Stadium within thirty seconds of when they are hit. On this one he took his time. "I needed to see a replay, but all the local broadcast showed was the ball falling out of the sky, not where it hit," Vuch recalls. "The ushers out in the stands verified that it hit that sign [an advertisement below luxury boxes in straightaway center field]. And then the Marlins' television replay confirmed that it did hit the sign."

Using the grid that takes into account the trajectory of the shot along with the configuration of the ballpark, Vuch finally posted the estimated distance in the bottom of the sixth. The ball, he estimated, had traveled a whopping 545 feet, the longest homer ever hit at Busch Stadium.

There are many physicists and students of human anatomy that doubt a human can hit a baseball as far as McGwire and others have hit. They believe that even the computers exaggerate the figures. They demand accuracy. They crave more realistic numbers. But baseball is not only a game of numbers, it is a game of myth. And the home run is baseball's most mythical feat. Take away the myth and you take away much of its magic.

There were no cameras. No computers. Not much coverage at all in the 1930s when the Pittsburgh Crawfords of the old Negro Leagues were playing at Pittsburgh's Forbes Field. On the Crawfords was Josh Gibson, one of the most prolific and strongest power hitters of all time. In that game—we don't even have a documented date—it is said that Gibson hit a home run so far it disappeared from view. The next day, however, the Crawfords were playing in Philadelphia and a ball fell out of the sky, landing in the glove of a very surprised Philadelphia center fielder. The umpire from the previous day saw the catch, pointed to Gibson, and yelled, "Yer out!"

Of course, Gibson's legendary feat can never be proven. We'll never know for sure if he actually hit that ball from Pittsburgh to Philadelphia. And if someone comes up with facts that dispute the feat, well, as the saying goes, and it applies to baseball and home runs, when the legend becomes fact, print the legend.

After a Mark McGwire home run struck a sign above center field at Busch Stadium, a Band-Aid was placed on the sign. The home run was estimated at 545 feet from home plate, the longest ever hit at Busch Stadium.

MINIMAL BLASTS

The tape-measure home run is well documented, but in all our glorification of power and strength, we sometimes forget what is an equally impressive deed: the inside-the-park home run. Statistics on the inside-the-park homer are just now being compiled. A home run is, after all, a home run and whether the ball cleared the fence or not was never, in the past, specified. Of the facts that have been compiled, we do know that there are some legendary tape-measure homer hitters who also legged out a few inside-the-park homers.

On August 11, 1923, at Detroit, Babe Ruth hit an inside-the-park home run, but what made the event even more memorable was that the next batter, Elmer Smith, followed by duplicating Ruth's deed.

104

Since 1884, according to still somewhat incomplete records, there have been 33 back-to-back inside the park home runs, but the only time that freakish occurrence has taken place since 1949 was on August 27, 1977 when Toby Harrah and Bump Wills of the Texas Rangers did it against the New York Yankees at Yankee Stadium.

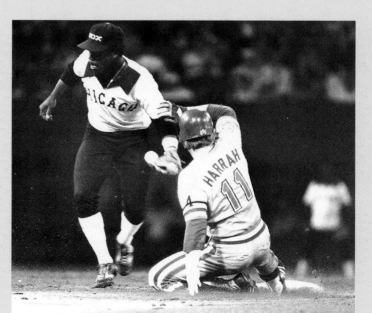

Toby Harrah (left) and Bump Wills (above) of the Texas Rangers hit back-to-back inside-the-park home runs in a game against the Yankees in 1977.

Another slugger who could run the bases was Dick Allen. And on July 31, 1972, during his MVP year playing for the Chicago White Sox, Allen hit two inside-the-park home runs in one game. With that accomplishment, Allen became the first player since 1950 to hit two inside-the-park home runs in one game. Allen's remarkable feat has since been duplicated three times including, on September 16, 1996, in different games, by two players: Ken Caminiti and Sammy Sosa.

The player with the most career inside-the-park home runs is Jesse Burkett with 56. Burkett played from 1890 until 1905, an era when parks were large and home runs over the fence were less likely than those within the stadium confines.

It's harder these days to circle the bases with the ball remaining in the park, but of the modern day players, Willie Wilson, who played fifteen years with the Kansas City Royals, has hit the most. The speedy Wilson hit 13 inside-the-park homers, the most by any one player since World War II.

(Above) Though statistics on inside-the-park home runs are vague, Jesse Burkett, above, holds the career lead with 56.

(Left) Willie Wilson smiles with glee as he slides safely into home after hitting one of his 13 career inside-the-park home runs in a game against the Milwaukee Brewers in 1979.

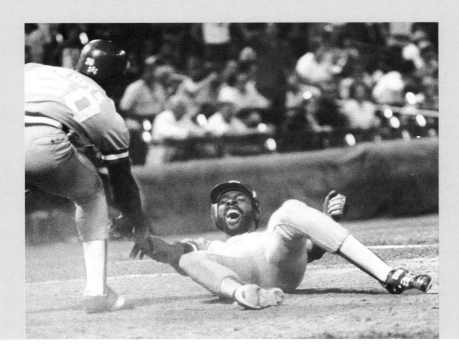

HOME RUN
DERBY

Ed Linn

Ed Linn, who died on February 7, 2000, at the age of 77, had a writing career that spanned almost half a century. He had the rare talent of being both an estimable reporter as well as a stellar writer. We are honored to have his words in this volume, but saddened that they are his last.

(Opposite) Babe Ruth and Lou Gehrig: teammates and the home run derby combatants of 1927.

There have been three great Home Run Derbies in Major League Baseball . . . okay, make it three and a half. Ruth-Gehrig in 1927; Maris-Mantle in 1961; McGwire-Sosa in 1998 and 1999.

The term Home Run Derby was coined for the unprecedented race between Ruth and Gehrig. There has never been anything like it and there can never be anything like it again because there can never again be a hitter who personified the home run like Babe Ruth.

In 1920, when Ruth hit 54 home runs he was almost doubling the record of 29 he had set the previous season in Boston. So complete was his domination that he had hit one out of every 6.8 home runs in the American League.

The next year he hit 59.

By 1927, Babe was thirty-two years old, and while he was still hitting twice as many balls out of the park as anybody else, it was clear that age and a life of high and joyful living were taking their inevitable toll.

Lou Gehrig was twenty-three and had shown some power by hitting 16 home runs the previous season and 20 the year before that.

Since the gods of drama always smiled benevolently upon the Babe, Gehrig's emergence as a serious challenger and Babe's final triumph both took place in Boston where he was still being looked upon as a beloved son who had been stolen away.

Gehrig had got off to a fast start by hitting four home runs in the first week, but by the time they came to Boston for a five-game series in June, Babe had reasserted his preeminence and was leading Gehrig,

22–17. Lou hit his eighteenth in the opening game and Babe fired back with two monstrous drives that went completely out of the park. The second one, which was estimated at 500 feet, was hailed by the Boston press as the longest home run ever hit at Fenway Park.

The next day, Gehrig hit *three*. He had already hit more home runs than he ever had before, and he was only three behind the Babe. But it was more than that. All three were monumental blasts, the first going as far as Ruth's 500-footer of the previous day, the other two landing in the center-field bleachers where only Ruth himself had ever reached before. Not even the Babe had ever done it twice in a single game. The message going forth was that Lou Gehrig had come to stay. The message was that the *home run* was no longer the copyrighted property of Babe Ruth.

A week later, when Gehrig hit two more home runs against the

108

After smacking two home runs in a July Fourth, 1927 double-header, sportswriters were, prematurely, calling Lou Gehrig (left) the "new home run king."

Red Sox in Yankee Stadium, he was not only two ahead of Ruth but was on a pace to break the Babe's record.

And so it was that on the Fourth of July, the largest crowd in New York baseball history—72,641—stormed Yankee Stadium to watch the home run twins in a doubleheader against the league-leading Washington Senators. And once again it was Gehrig who stole the show with a three-run home run off Walter Johnson in the first game, and a grand slam home run deep into the right-center bleachers in the second.

He hit them as far as Babe had, he hit them as often, and he was nine years younger. The New York sportswriters, having already dubbed them "Bam and Buster," unhesitatingly crowned Lou Gehrig the new home run king.

The Yankees headed west and home run mania gripped the nation. Record crowds greeted them everywhere. For a Saturday double-

Ruth (below) kept pace with Gehrig by not only hitting as many home runs, but by hitting them farther than anyone could ever imagine.

109

header in Detroit, the Tigers' management installed temporary stands in the huge expanse of their center-field area and they still had to rope off the outfield to accommodate the overflow.

Babe hit two into the temporary stands, mighty blows both, but not home runs on any other day of the season. Take away those two home runs and Babe would not have broken the record, would he?

With radio in its infancy, word had to be flashed to newspapers around the country via telegraph key. "There has never been anything like it," wrote Paul Gallico. "Even as these lines are batted out on the office typewriter, youths dash out of the wire service ticker room every two or three minutes shouting, 'Ruth just hit one. Gehrig just hit another one.'"

And then the most astonishing thing of all happened. With a day off between St. Louis and Chicago, the Yankees had scheduled an exhibition game in St. Paul. At every railroad station between St. Louis and St. Paul, through the night and into the early morning hours, there would be people waiting for the Yankees' train to pass. Ruth would come out to the platform and make a little speech and then drag the shy Gehrig out of bed to mumble a few words.

Fifty thousand people filled Comiskey Park for the opening game in Chicago. Comiskey Park had been rebuilt that year. The fences had been moved back, double-decked bleachers had been installed. The architect had offered a public guarantee that no mere mortal would ever be able to hit a baseball completely out of the park.

Babe Ruth didn't quite hit it out. All he was able to do was hit the longest ball ever hit within the city limits of Chicago, a line drive into the farthest reaches of the upper right-field stands. He surpassed that a month later when the Yankees came back to Chicago by hitting the ball completely out of the park. The blow so ignited the crowd that the police had to rescue him from the fans who engulfed him before he was able to complete his tour around the bases.

Back and forth they went. Two players on the same team, hitting back to back. Ruth would go ahead, Gehrig would shake his hand as he crossed the plate and hit another one to tie him again. Twenty-one times during the season they were tied.

When they returned to Boston in September, Ruth was holding a 44–43 lead, and excitement was at such a high pitch that traffic was at a complete standstill at Kenmore Square; announcements were being made at the train station and subway stop that anybody who didn't have a ticket should turn around and go home. Disappointed fans surrounded the park and an untold number broke through the outfield fences in two places, forcing the Boston management to rope off the outfield.

Lou Gehrig hit his 44th home run in the opener, the twentieth time they had been tied during the season. In the second game, the Babe began to take over. It didn't seem that way in the beginning, though. In the first inning, Gehrig hit his 45th to take the lead. Ruth came up in the third and hit what was once again called the longest home run ever hit in Boston. "The ball was still climbing when it went high over the highest part of the high fence in center field, just to the left of the flagpole. Nobody at the park could tell where it landed."

Gehrig had gone ahead of Ruth for about twenty minutes. He was going to remain tied for about the same length of time. The next time up, Ruth hit a 3–0 pitch into the right-field stands to take back the lead.

His third home run of the day was hit in the final inning of the second game. "Only the fresh memory of #45," the *Boston Herald* informed its readers, "prevented the enthusiastic fans from labeling #47 the greatest ever."

The next day he hit two more. The Babe was leading 49–45, and the wind just seemed to go out of Gehrig's sails.

To break the record, Babe needed 11 home runs in 25 games.

The 56th is notable because it came in the ninth inning and won the game. Since the game was over the moment he hit the ball, he took the precaution of carrying his bat around the bases with him. A kid running out as Babe was rounding third grabbed the bat. And Babe—who else would have done this?—dragged the boy and bat across the plate with him.

The record-breaker came on the next to last day of the season in his last at-bat against Tom Zachary to break a 2–2 tie. He golfed a curving drive that landed halfway up in the bleachers.

Lou Gehrig didn't hit his 47th until the final day of the season.

Ruth gets a handshake from Gehrig after another home run. By September of '27, he took the home run lead from his teammate for good.

111

The M & M boys, Mickey Mantle, left, and Roger Maris, right, hold their shirts together to form the combined number of home runs they hit in 1960: Mantle with 40, Maris with 39. That number would dramatically increase in 1961.

112

The Mantle-Maris race in 1961 was a repeat of 1927, with the number three and number four hitters of the New York Yankees engaging in a back-to-back, seesawing Home Run Derby. In both instances, the number three hitter won. The great difference was that Maris was no Ruth. Another difference was that Maris was so well protected by having Mantle batting behind him that not once in his whole record-breaking season was Roger passed intentionally.

What was so special about 1961? Well, Ted Williams and Casey Stengel, the two foremost gate attractions in the American League, had left the scene at the end of the 1960 season, after what had been two lackluster

seasons characterized by a lamentable dearth of power hitters.

Roger Maris was the wrong man to break the record of Babe Ruth. If it was going to be anybody it should have been Mickey Mantle, a certified home run hitter. Like Ruth and Gehrig, Mantle hit long, high-riding home runs. Like Ruth and Gehrig, Mantle not only knocked in runs but hit over .300 regularly. Roger Maris was a great all-around player (as if anybody cared about that) but he was also little better than a .260 hitter.

What Maris did have was a swing that was made for Yankee Stadium. Not gargantuan drives but fly balls that were long enough to reach the right-field bleachers. In his first year with the Yankees he had hit 39 home runs to finish second to Mantle's 40.

In his year of glory, Maris got off to such a dismal start that midway through May he had hit only 3 home runs to Mantle's 10.

But then he got so hot through the rest of May and the month of June that by the time of the All-Star break he was leading Mantle, 33–29, and both were on a pace to break the Babe's record. (If all the hitters who had been on a pace to break the Babe's record in July were laid end to end, they would cover a three-lane highway to Cooperstown.) But something else was happening in 1961. The American League had expanded from eight teams to ten, and eight extra games had been added to the schedule.

The question that was therefore vexing the best minds in the press box was whether either of them could be credited with breaking Babe's record if he had hit less than 60 home runs in the first 154 games. While they were about it, the New York writers did their best

113

Roger Maris and his swing that was made for Yankee Stadium.

to spice up their coverage by fabricating a feud between them.

Actually, Mickey and Roger lived together in New York and got along famously. Maris, an early riser, would come back with the morning paper, wake Mickey up, and say, "Hey, roomie, you've got to read this. We're fighting again."

Like Ruth and Gehrig, they seemed to feed off each other. In the week after the All-Star game, Mantle went off on an 8 home run tear to take the lead, just as everybody had expected. The first indication that Maris was not going to go away came in Chicago a week later. In his first time at bat, Maris hit a home run off the right-field foul pole to go back into a tie. Whereupon Mantle hit a home run off the left-field foul pole to go back out in front. There was nothing freakish about what happened the following day, though, as Maris hit three home runs in a Saturday doubleheader.

The press and the fans were rooting for Mantle, here connecting on one of his 56 homers in 1961, to be the one to break the Babe's record.

114

Now it was Maris with 40—more than he had ever hit before—and Mantle with 38, almost a reverse of their final totals the previous year. And there were still two months left in the season. And suddenly, everybody was rooting for Mantle, the old hero. Mantle had the *standing* to break Babe Ruth's record. Maris didn't. Roger Maris was like a high jumper who had never jumped over 6′3″ before and was suddenly clearing the bar at 6′10″ and threatening to reach the magic 7 feet.

For all intents and purposes, Maris won the crown late in August when he hit seven home runs in successive series against Washington and Chicago under the most illogical of circumstances.

Washington had always been a jinxed park for him. On his last visit to Griffith Stadium, the Senators had thrown an extreme shift against him, placing three infielders on the right side of the diamond, and Roger had gone hitless through the entire series. This time he was in a terrible slump, with only one home run in 16 games. The only comforting thing to him, he confessed, was that it was going to be the last time he would ever have to play in Griffith Stadium because the Senators were about to move to Municipal Stadium.

So naturally he hit home runs on four successive days, and, with Mantle matching him in the first and third games, they were tied again at 45.

115

Maris and Mantle with Mrs. Babe Ruth at Yankee Stadium in 1961.

He wasn't supposed to hit left-handers either, and so back in New York against the White Sox he took the lead with a home run off a tough, fast-balling lefty, Juan Pizarro, and gave himself a cushion the next day—which was Babe Ruth Day in Yankee Stadium—with two home runs off an even tougher left-hander, Billy Pierce.

And then it was over. With 19 games left in the season, Mantle was knocked out of the lineup by a bad case of flu. He did play one game in Boston at the end of the road trip and hit a 3-run home run, but on the way back to New York, Mel Allen, the Yankees' announcer, told him about a doctor who had cured him and many of his friends of similar afflictions with a "miracle" injection. The doctor gave Mickey the injection and the next day Mickey was in the hospital with a raging fever and a deep infection.

The race had come down to Roger Maris versus the ghost of Babe Ruth. The 154th game was played in Baltimore, the one park where he had not hit a home run. Not officially, anyway. Earlier in the season, Roger and Mickey had both had home runs washed away when the game was rained out after four and two-thirds innings. When Roger insisted that his only disappointment was that the Yankees had lost what had looked like a sure victory, a disbelieving reporter had asked, "But what if you only have 59 home runs after 154 games?"

"I'll ask for a raise," said Roger.

In the 154th game of the season, Roger Maris hit his 59th home run in Baltimore.

The 60th came against Jack Fisher, the same pitcher who had thrown the home run ball to Ted Williams in his last time at bat the previous season. There were four games left for Maris to break the Babe's record: a final game against Baltimore and a three-game series with Boston.

(Above) Maris watches as the ball he has just hit clears the Yankee Stadium fences for his 60th and record-tying home run on September 26th.

(Opposite) October 1, 1961, Maris hits a "typical Maris home run," but this, number 61 for the year, breaks the hallowed record set by Babe Ruth 34 years earlier.

The pressure of the whole season, climaxing in the run up to Babe Ruth's 60, had been so great that Roger sat himself down for the Baltimore game to give himself a chance to relax and regroup. And that left three games.

What made Roger's day off so remarkable was that the Baltimore pitchers had been willing to challenge him in these late-season games and the Red Sox pitchers had been making him chase bad pitches.

For two days, the Red Sox pitchers gave him nothing to hit. On the final day, a smallish crowd of 23,154 showed up on a warm Sunday afternoon to find out whether Roger Maris—who wasn't either Mickey Mantle or Babe Ruth—was going to break baseball's most hallowed record.

Pitching for the Red Sox was a rookie right-hander, Tracy Stallard. On the first time at bat, Maris swung at a pitch outside the strike zone and flied out to left field. In the fourth inning, the first two pitches were balls, and the Yankee players were up on the dugout stairs yelling, "Give him something he can swing at. . . . Give him something

116

he can hit." The next pitch was a fast ball on the outside corner, not a bad pitch but a pitch that Maris could handle. It was a typical Maris home run: a long fly that landed ten rows high in the right-field bleachers.

The final score was 1–0.

CHASING A GHOST

Henry Aaron did everything quietly and smoothly. Seemingly without effort. But also without flair.

He was a great hitter, a great fielder, a great base runner, and he had a great arm. But mostly he was a hitter. He had such a short, quick, compact swing that his bat seemed to flick out at the ball like the tongue of a snake.

The only thing colorful about him was his home run trot. He would hold his elbows up high and kind of swagger from the waist up while he was kind of shuffling from the waist down. And though he wasn't setting any single-season home run records, he was taking that home run trot at a consistently high rate.

118

Hank Aaron hitting his 715th home run on April 8, 1974.

And so in 1973—his twentieth year with the Milwaukee-Atlanta Braves—it became apparent that Henry Aaron had been steadily crawling up on Babe Ruth's absolutely, positively unbreakable record of 714 home runs.

As the 1973 season came to an end, his total had reached 713. One short.

It didn't take long. On his first swing of the 1974 season, Hank Aaron lined a 3–1 pitch from Cincinnati's Jack Billingham into the left-field stands.

He wanted to break the record before the hometown fans, though, and on opening day in Atlanta-Fulton County Stadium, before a crowd of 52,780, his bat flicked out at a low fastball from the veteran Al Downing and the ball landed in the left-field bullpen.

He had done it on his first swing of the bat there, too.

As he rounded the bases, Aaron admitted to being in his own little world. "It was like running in a bubble and I could see all these people jumping up and down and waving their arms in slow motion."

Called back to home plate and handed a microphone, Hank Aaron said only: "I just thank God it's all over."

119

The new home run king of all time tips his cap to his teammates as they await his arrival at home plate.

The home run record in 1998 was not exactly unexpected. The year before, Mark McGwire had hit 58 home runs in his split season between Oakland and St. Louis, and the eyes of the entire baseball world were on him. In the first two weeks of the season, he had 8 home runs, three of them coming in a single game against Arizona. In the month of May he had 16 home runs, including two 2 home run games and yet another 3-homer game. In one week alone, he hit 8 home runs.

"Hit it out of the park and they will come," the Lords of Baseball were praying. Not only were they coming in record numbers, they were coming out early to watch McGwire launch his moon shots in batting practice. Big Mac had always hit for great distances. But now his distances were otherworldly.

120

Mark McGwire, here legging out another homer, came close to the single season home run record in 1997, hitting 58, but no one was prepared for what was to come in 1998.

Meanwhile, Sosa was back in the middle of the pack behind half a dozen of the other big boppers. He didn't come as a complete surprise like Maris had, but he shouldn't have been a surprise at all. In 1996, he had 40 home runs in 124 games before a broken bone in his hand put him out for the season.

By mid-June, McGwire had hit 31 balls out of the park, and Sosa had hit 20.

And then McGwire slackened off. He began to grouse about all the attention, the same questions being asked in every new city, the infestation of writers from all over the country. The suspicion began to be voiced around baseball that Mark McGwire did not have the temperament to withstand the pressure.

And then along came Sammy Sosa. Big Mac had hit 16 homers in May? Sosa hit 20 in June. In one nine-day stretch he had ten home runs, including a 3 home run game of his own against Milwaukee and consecutive 2-homer days against the Phillies. Just like that, Sosa had 30 home runs to McGwire's 33.

Nothing bothered Sammy. Sammy was loose. Sammy was fun. Sammy was exactly the offset that McGwire needed. By the All-Star break Big Mac had 40 home runs in 90 games. Unbelievable. So unbelievable that Sosa's 35, which was also well ahead of Roger Maris's pace, went practically unnoticed.

After a hundred games, McGwire was coasting along with a lead of 43–37, and once again it looked like clear sailing ahead.

And once again . . . here came Sosa! Never during the season was Sosa ahead when the day came to an end. But never was McGwire able to shake him.

By August 8, Sammy was only two homers behind. Two days later he hit two home runs to defeat San Francisco in extra innings, and for the first time all season he had tied McGwire at 46. The next day, McGwire went back out ahead. A day after that, Sosa had tied him again.

To make it perfect—ah, how lucky those schedule-makers can be—the Cardinals were coming to

By the end of May, Sammy Sosa only had 11 home runs to Mark McGwire's 27.

121

In June, Sosa went on a tear, whacking a remarkable 20 homers in 27 games. By the end of June, he had 33 home runs to McGwire's 37.

Wrigley Field, and the two combatants were going to meet head-to-head. A clash of giants. And for once a highly-publicized confrontation was going to live up to its billing.

In the fifth inning, Sosa sent the Chicago fans into paroxysms of joy by rapping out his 48th home run to go ahead of Big Mac for the first time. But not for long. Three innings later, McGwire hit the ball over everything in sight to send the game into extra innings. And then hit his 49th in the tenth inning to win it.

They were going to be meeting one last time at Busch Stadium, seventeen days later, and it was going to be even better.

Lou Gehrig had faded away over the last three weeks in 1927. Mickey Mantle had been knocked out of the lineup by illness in 1961. McGwire and Sosa were going down to the wire in 1998.

It was always McGwire drawing away from Sosa, and Sosa very quickly closing the gap. Sosa would hit one in a day game. McGwire would match it that same night. Sosa would hit two home runs one day; McGwire would hit two home runs the next. On twenty-one separate occasions, they hit home runs on the same day.

On the last day of August, with 25 games left to be played, Sosa hit a home run off Cincinnati's Brett Tomko to tie it again at 55.

What captivated everybody, what made the race for the record so great, was that they liked each other, admired each other, enjoyed each other.

If McGwire was The Man—as Sosa kept saying—then Sammy was the catalyst. In the season of his life, Sammy Sosa was having the time of his life. The ritual he went through became familiar. After every home run he would return to the bench and, walking toward the TV camera, he would thump his heart, place two fingers to his lips, bring the fingers out into a V sign to his mother back in the Dominican Republic and whisper, "I love you, Mama."

McGwire raises his arms in triumph after hitting his 61st home run to tie Roger Maris's record.

Each of them had his signature reaction to a home run. Sosa would slap his hands together and do a little sideways skip toward first base before going into his home run trot. McGwire would raise his arms like a conquering hero (a little *Rocky* music here, professor) before settling into his big-footed run around the bases.

When they met for that final time in St. Louis—the most dramatic possible scenario has a way of writing itself, doesn't it?—Big Red had his 60 home runs and was perched upon the brink of Maris's record.

At a delightful, nationally televised press conference before the first of the two games, Sosa was still casting

123

The two home run kings of 1998 hug and mug before a game.

McGwire as "The Man" and refusing to even consider the possibility that he could beat him.

"Wouldn't it be great if we tied," said McGwire. "I think it would be beautiful."

"Tied at what?" asked a reporter.

"Seventy would be good," said McGwire.

"I'll take it," grinned Sosa.

It was also a great time for family values. McGwire had his ten-year-old son, Matt, there as bat boy so that he could witness, share, and always remember his father's greatest moment.

He also had Maris's six grown children there to keep the memory of Roger Maris alive.

He didn't keep them waiting either day. Number 61 came on Mike Morgan's third pitch in the first inning on September 7. The record-breaking 62nd came the next day, September 8, on the first pitch of his second time at bat. It was a line shot off Steve Trachsel that just made it over the left-field fence near the foul line, 341 feet away, the shortest and most atypical McGwire home run of the year.

Around the bases went Big Mac, shaking hands and high-fiving the Cubs' infielders, and when he reached home plate he lifted his not-so-little son high up off the ground in a crushing, if rather awkward, bear hug.

Sosa trotted in from right field to congratulate him, and they went through their familiar ritual in which McGwire would fake a punch to the stomach, and Sosa would give his two-finger "I love you" salute to both Mac and the crowd. After faking the punch, McGwire hoisted Sosa in a bear hug, too. And then McGwire went into the grandstand to embrace Maris's children.

But the Home Run Derby wasn't over. When he hit the record-breaking 62nd home run, he was ahead of Sosa by four, and there were 18 games still left.

September 8, 1998, Mark McGwire's line drive clears the left-field fence at Busch Stadium for his 62nd home run of the season.

125

126

Sosa leaping in the air after hitting his 62nd homer on September 13th. By September 23rd, he and McGwire were tied at 65.

Before it was over, the old pattern was going to reassert itself one more time.

There were still 12 games to go when Sosa hit his 62nd and became the co-holder of the new record. McGwire sat out the next game but came up in the ninth inning and hit a pinch-hit home run to set a new record at 63. Sosa caught him a day later with a grand slam home run in San Diego and was rewarded by a fireworks display and a standing ovation that left the Padres players enraged.

With every home run setting a new record, McGwire went two

ahead in the 156th game of the season. Sosa hit two in the Cubs' 159th game to tie him at 65.

Two days later, Sammy Sosa hit his 66th in Wrigley Field to take the lead for the second time. For the next forty-five minutes, Sammy Sosa, the former shoeshine boy from the Dominican Republic, had hit more home runs in a single season than anybody who had ever played the game. Then Big Red hit a monster home run in St. Louis against Montreal and—with two games remaining—they were tied again at 66. A perfect ending, one would have thought. Wasn't it McGwire who had been saying that a tie would be beautiful?

"Beautiful" was great. "Awesome" was even better.

In each of those last two games, Big Mac crushed two home runs to finish with a perfectly round 70.

He had started the season with four home runs in the first four games. He ended it with five home runs in the last three.

McGwire, here culminating a home run frenzy in the final weekend of the 1998 season and the last game of the year by hitting his 70th.

CATCHING FAME

We've just read the stories of those momentous feats, but they weren't the only ones who will go down in the record books. The lucky few who caught the balls are also, now, mini-celebrities themselves. Here are their stories.

OCTOBER 1, 1961: MARIS'S 61ST

Sal Durante, a nineteen-year-old auto-parts store worker from Brooklyn, had made a last-minute decision that morning to attend the final regular game of the season at Yankee Stadium with his fiancée, Rosemarie. "My dream since I was a kid was just to get a baseball, a batting practice baseball," Durante said. "That's why we asked for seats in right field. I wasn't really thinking about Roger and the record." The large concentration of fans certainly were when Roger Maris rocked Red Sox pitcher Tracy Stallard's pitch fifteen rows into the right-field stands. "As soon as it was hit, I knew it was going over my head," Durante said. "So I jumped on my seat and reached as high as I could . . . [the ball] hit the palm of my hand, like my hand was a magnet. It knocked me over into the next row." Enthusiastically swinging his arm to show that he had held on, Durante was helped to his feet by security guards and escorted off to meet the new home run champ. "I was amazed, in shock," Durante said. "All I could think of was I wanted to give the ball to Roger. I didn't care about anything else. I wanted Roger to have it." But Maris refused to accept his 61st home run ball. "Roger said, 'Make yourself some money,'" Durante said. The nineteen-year-old Coney Island resident, who was making sixty dollars a week at the auto-supply place, received five thousand dollars from a California restaurateur (who later donated the ball to the Hall of Fame) and an all-expenses-paid honeymoon out West. Durante, who works as a bus driver, now lives on Staten Island with his wife, Rosemarie.

Roger Maris with young Sal Durante who caught his 61st home run ball.

128

APRIL 8, 1974: HENRY AARON'S 715TH

Out in the bullpen at Atlanta Fulton-County Stadium, the Braves relief corps decided to assign twenty-foot-wide lanes for each player to patrol in case the historic home run ball didn't reach the stands. Because Aaron was a pull hitter, the veterans got the choice sections nearest to the left-field line, the less experienced players closer to center field. On Dodger pitcher Al Downing's second pitch in the fourth inning, Aaron hammered the ball just beyond the left-center-field fence, where fourth-year lefty Tom House was lucky to be standing. After the record-breaking 715th home run ball landed in House's glove, he sprinted from the pen to home plate, where he

presented the prize to the new career leader. "That's my claim to fame," House said. "I'm a question in Trivial Pursuit, and my picture with Henry is in the Hall of Fame." House closed out an eight-year Major League career with a 29–23 record and 33 saves before becoming a respected pitching coach (most recently with the Texas Rangers).

Hank Aaron holds up the 715th home run ball he hit that was caught in the bullpen by Atlanta relief pitcher Tom House.

129

SEPTEMBER 27, 1998: MCGWIRE'S 70TH

At 3:20 P.M., about a hundred coworkers from the Washington University research lab were enjoying an outing at Busch Stadium that had been planned far in advance. In their private party box beyond the left-field fence, a hard-hit baseball off the bat of Mark McGwire came flying through the open area, and half a dozen scientists scrambled for it. Phil Ozersky, a twenty-six-year-old geneticist from Olivette, Missouri, came away with the prize. "I went to a ball game, and all of a sudden there are millions of dollars in my hand." After the sale, licensing, and endorsement deals net out, Ozersky will net a record three million dollars for the historic 70th home run souvenir. (Prior to that, the highest price ever paid for a baseball was $500,000 for Eddie Murray's 500th home run ball, followed by the $126,500 shelled out for the first home run ever hit in Yankee Stadium— by Babe Ruth.) Ozersky still works at Washington University for an annual salary of about thirty thousand dollars.

THE *REAL* HOME RUN DERBY

Imagine Mickey Mantle and Willie Mays facing off in their prime, swinging away on every pitch for all the marbles. Or Hank Aaron and Eddie Mathews, slugging head to head. Or Frank Robinson and Dick Stuart, matching power against power. Or how about Harmon Killebrew and Rocky Colavito, stepping up to the plate to trade cuts. It happened in 1960, not as an added attraction at All-Star Game time, but as a thirty-minute prime-time offering every week.

Rocky Colavito

Home Run Derby, the syndicated TV show hosted and produced by Mark Scott, paired the top sluggers of the era in mano-a-mano competition: nine innings, three outs per inning; anything other than a homer or a ball was an out (including a called strike by the plate umpire); the winner received two thousand dollars (the loser one thousand) and an opportunity to defend his "crown" against a new challenger on the following week's show. In addition, a player who hit three consecutive home runs got a five hundred dollar bonus, another five hundred if he hit four in a row, and a thousand dollars for five or more straight dingers. It was big bucks back then, even for superstars, and nineteen of the biggest boppers in the game—including nine future Hall of Famers—were happy and grateful to participate.

Dick Stuart

Until his eclipse by Wally Post after six straight victories, Hammerin' Hank Aaron fittingly set the program's total-earnings mark with $13,500—more than any previous individual World Series share. (Mickey Mantle finished second in prize money with $10,000.) During Aaron's record-setting run, Mark Scott remarked to the future all-time circuit-clout leader: "Hank, you're making a career of *Home Run Derby*."

Alas, the popular series lasted only one season: six months after filming the twenty-sixth and final episode, Scott died of a heart attack. However, the classic shows (and swings) can still be seen in black-and-white reruns.

131

HOME RUN STATISTICS

Compiled by Elias Sports Bureau

ANNUAL HOME RUN LEADERS 1900–1999

(Opposite) The Babe and his arsenal of bats.

AMERICAN LEAGUE

YEAR	NAME	TEAM	HRs
1900 League Not Yet Formed			
1901	Nap Lajoie	Philadelphia Athletics	14
1902	Socks Seybold	Philadelphia Athletics	16
1903	Buck Freeman	Boston Pilgrims	13
1904	Harry Davis	Philadelphia Athletics	10
1905	Harry Davis	Philadelphia Athletics	8
1906	Harry Davis	Philadelphia Athletics	12
1907	Harry Davis	Philadelphia Athletics	8
1908	Sam Crawford	Detroit Tigers	7
1909	Ty Cobb	Detroit Tigers	9
1910	Jake Stahl	Boston Red Sox	10
1911	Frank Baker	Philadelphia Athletics	11
1912	Frank Baker	Philadelphia Athletics	10
	Tris Speaker	Boston Red Sox	10
1913	Frank Baker	Philadelphia Athletics	12
1914	Frank Baker	Philadelphia Athletics	9
1915	Braggo Roth	Chicago White Sox/Cleveland	7
1916	Wally Pipp	New York Yankees	12
1917	Wally Pipp	New York Yankees	9
1918	Babe Ruth	Boston Red Sox	11
	Tilly Walker	Philadelphia Athletics	11
1919	Babe Ruth	Boston Red Sox	29
1920	Babe Ruth	New York Yankees	54
1921	Babe Ruth	New York Yankees	59
1922	Ken Williams	St. Louis Browns	39

AMERICAN LEAGUE [CONTINUED]

YEAR	NAME	TEAM	HRs
1923	Babe Ruth	New York Yankees	41
1924	Babe Ruth	New York Yankees	46
1925	Bob Meusel	New York Yankees	33
1926	Babe Ruth	New York Yankees	47
1927	Babe Ruth	New York Yankees	60
1928	Babe Ruth	New York Yankees	54
1929	Babe Ruth	New York Yankees	46
1930	Babe Ruth	New York Yankees	49
1931	Babe Ruth	New York Yankees	46
	Lou Gehrig	New York Yankees	46
1932	Jimmie Foxx	Philadelphia Athletics	58
1933	Jimmie Foxx	Philadelphia Athletics	48
1934	Lou Gehrig	New York Yankees	49
1935	Jimmie Foxx	Philadelphia Athletics	36
	Hank Greenberg	Detroit Tigers	36
1936	Lou Gehrig	New York Yankees	49
1937	Joe DiMaggio	New York Yankees	46
1938	Hank Greenberg	Detroit Tigers	58
1939	Jimmie Foxx	Boston Red Sox	35
1940	Hank Greenberg	Detroit Tigers	41
1941	Ted Williams	Boston Red Sox	37
1942	Ted Williams	Boston Red Sox	36
1943	Rudy York	Detroit Tigers	34
1944	Nick Etten	New York Yankees	22
1945	Vern Stephens	St. Louis Browns	24
1946	Hank Greenberg	Detroit Tigers	44
1947	Ted Williams	Boston Red Sox	32
1948	Joe DiMaggio	New York Yankees	39
1949	Ted Williams	Boston Red Sox	43
1950	Al Rosen	Cleveland Indians	37
1951	Gus Zernial	Chicago White Sox/ Philadelphia Athletics	33
1952	Larry Doby	Cleveland Indians	32
1953	Al Rosen	Cleveland Indians	43
1954	Larry Doby	Cleveland Indians	32
1955	Mickey Mantle	New York Yankees	37
1956	Mickey Mantle	New York Yankees	52

134

AMERICAN LEAGUE [CONTINUED]

YEAR	NAME	TEAM	HRs
1957	Roy Sievers	Washington Senators	42
1958	Mickey Mantle	New York Yankees	42
1959	Rocky Colavito	Cleveland Indians	42
	Harmon Killebrew	Washington Senators	42
1960	Mickey Mantle	New York Yankees	40
1961	Roger Maris	New York Yankees	61
1962	Harmon Killebrew	Minnesota Twins	48
1963	Harmon Killebrew	Minnesota Twins	45
1964	Harmon Killebrew	Minnesota Twins	49
1965	Tony Conigliaro	Boston Red Sox	32
1966	Frank Robinson	Baltimore Orioles	49
1967	Harmon Killebrew	Minnesota Twins	44
	Carl Yastrzemski	Boston Red Sox	44
1968	Frank Howard	Washington Senators	44
1969	Harmon Killebrew	Minnesota Twins	49
1970	Frank Howard	Washington Senators	44
1971	Bill Melton	Chicago White Sox	33
1972	Dick Allen	Chicago White Sox	37
1973	Reggie Jackson	Oakland Athletics	32
1974	Dick Allen	Chicago White Sox	32
1975	Reggie Jackson	Oakland Athletics	36
	George Scott	Milwaukee Brewers	36
1976	Graig Nettles	New York Yankees	32
1977	Jim Rice	Boston Red Sox	39
1978	Jim Rice	Boston Red Sox	46
1979	Gorman Thomas	Milwaukee Brewers	45
1980	Reggie Jackson	New York Yankees	41
	Ben Oglivie	Milwaukee Brewers	41
1981	Tony Armas	Oakland Athletics	22
	Dwight Evans	Boston Red Sox	22
	Bobby Grich	California Angels	22
	Eddie Murray	Baltimore Orioles	22
1982	Reggie Jackson	California Angels	39
	Gorman Thomas	Milwaukee Brewers	39
1983	Jim Rice	Boston Red Sox	39
1984	Tony Armas	Boston Red Sox	43
1985	Darrell Evans	Detroit Tigers	40

135

AMERICAN LEAGUE [CONTINUED]

YEAR	NAME	TEAM	HRs
1986	Jesse Barfield	Toronto Blue Jays	40
1987	Mark McGwire	Oakland Athletics	49
1988	Jose Canseco	Oakland Athletics	42
1989	Fred McGriff	Toronto Blue Jays	36
1990	Cecil Fielder	Detroit Tigers	51
1991	Jose Canseco	Oakland Athletics	44
	Cecil Fielder	Detroit Tigers	44
1992	Juan Gonzalez	Texas Rangers	43
1993	Juan Gonzalez	Texas Rangers	46
1994	Ken Griffey, Jr.	Seattle Mariners	40
1995	Albert Belle	Cleveland Indians	50
1996	Mark McGwire	Oakland Athletics	52
1997	Mark McGwire	Oakland Athletics/ St. Louis Cardinals	58
	Ken Griffey, Jr.	Seattle Mariners	56
1998	Ken Griffey, Jr.	Seattle Mariners	56
1999	Ken Griffey, Jr.	Seattle Mariners	48

136

Cecil Fielder hit 51 home runs in 1990, making him the first American Leaguer to hit more than 50 since 1961.

NATIONAL LEAGUE

YEAR	NAME	TEAM	HRs
1900	Herman Long	Boston Beaneaters	12
1901	Sam Crawford	Cincinnati Reds	16
1902	Tommy Leach	Pittsburgh Pirates	6
1903	Jimmy Sheckard	Brooklyn Superbas	9
1904	Harry Lumley	Brooklyn Superbas	9
1905	Fred Odwell	Cincinnati Reds	9
1906	Tim Jordan	Brooklyn Dodgers	12
1907	Dave Brain	Boston Beaneaters	10
1908	Tim Jordan	Brooklyn Dodgers	12
1909	Red Murray	New York Giants	7
1910	Fred Beck	Boston Beaneaters	10
	Wildfire Schulte	Chicago Cubs	10
1911	Wildfire Schulte	Chicago Cubs	21
1912	Heinie Zimmerman	Chicago Cubs	14
1913	Gavvy Cravath	Philadelphia Phillies	19
1914	Gavvy Cravath	Philadelphia Phillies	19
1915	Gavvy Cravath	Philadelphia Phillies	24
1916	Dave Robertson	New York Giants	12
	Cy Williams	Chicago Cubs	12
1917	Gavvy Cravath	Philadelphia Phillies	12
	Dave Robertson	New York Giants	12
1918	Gavvy Cravath	Philadelphia Phillies	8
1919	Gavvy Cravath	Philadelphia Phillies	12
1920	Cy Williams	Philadelphia Phillies	15
1921	George Kelly	New York Giants	23
1922	Rogers Hornsby	St. Louis Cardinals	42
1923	Cy Williams	Philadelphia Phillies	41
1924	Jack Fournier	Brooklyn Dodgers	27
1925	Rogers Hornsby	St. Louis Cardinals	39
1926	Hack Wilson	Chicago Cubs	21
1927	Hack Wilson	Chicago Cubs	30
	Cy Williams	Philadelphia Phillies	30
1928	Hack Wilson	Chicago Cubs	31
	Jim Bottomley	St. Louis Cardinals	31
1929	Chuck Klein	Philadelphia Phillies	43
1930	Hack Wilson	Chicago Cubs	56
1931	Chuck Klein	Philadelphia Phillies	31

NATIONAL LEAGUE [CONTINUED]

YEAR	NAME	TEAM	HRs
1932	Mel Ott	New York Giants	38
	Chuck Klein	Philadelphia Phillies	38
1933	Chuck Klein	Philadelphia Phillies	28
1934	Ripper Collins	St. Louis Cardinals	35
	Mel Ott	New York Giants	35
1935	Wally Berger	Boston Braves	34
1936	Mel Ott	New York Giants	33
1937	Joe Medwick	St. Louis Cardinals	31
	Mel Ott	New York Giants	31
1938	Mel Ott	New York Giants	36
1939	Johnny Mize	St. Louis Cardinals	28
1940	Johnny Mize	St. Louis Cardinals	43
1941	Dolph Camilli	Brooklyn Dodgers	34
1942	Mel Ott	New York Giants	30
1943	Bill Nicholson	Chicago Cubs	29
1944	Bill Nicholson	Chicago Cubs	33
1945	Tommy Holmes	Boston Braves	28
1946	Ralph Kiner	Pittsburgh Pirates	23
1947	Ralph Kiner	Pittsburgh Pirates	51
	Johnny Mize	New York Giants	51

138

Ralph Kiner tied or led the National League in homers for seven consecutive seasons from 1946 through 1952.

NATIONAL LEAGUE [CONTINUED]

YEAR	NAME	TEAM	HRs
1948	Ralph Kiner	Pittsburgh Pirates	40
	Johnny Mize	New York Giants	40
1949	Ralph Kiner	Pittsburgh Pirates	54
1950	Ralph Kiner	Pittsburgh Pirates	47
1951	Ralph Kiner	Pittsburgh Pirates	42
1952	Ralph Kiner	Pittsburgh Pirates	37
	Hank Sauer	Chicago Cubs	37
1953	Eddie Mathews	Milwaukee Braves	47
1954	Ted Kluszewski	Cincinnati Reds	49
1955	Willie Mays	New York Giants	51
1956	Duke Snider	Brooklyn Dodgers	43
1957	Hank Aaron	Milwaukee Braves	44
1958	Ernie Banks	Chicago Cubs	47
1959	Eddie Mathews	Milwaukee Braves	46
1960	Ernie Banks	Chicago Cubs	41
1961	Orlando Cepeda	San Francisco Giants	46
1962	Willie Mays	San Francisco Giants	49
1963	Hank Aaron	Milwaukee Braves	44
	Willie McCovey	San Francisco Giants	44
1964	Willie Mays	San Francisco Giants	47
1965	Willie Mays	San Francisco Giants	52
1966	Hank Aaron	Atlanta Braves	44
1967	Hank Aaron	Atlanta Braves	39
1968	Willie McCovey	San Francisco Giants	36
1969	Willie McCovey	San Francisco Giants	45
1970	Johnny Bench	Cincinnati Reds	45
1971	Willie Stargell	Pittsburgh Pirates	48
1972	Johnny Bench	Cincinnati Reds	40
1973	Willie Stargell	Pittsburgh Pirates	44
1974	Mike Schmidt	Philadelphia Phillies	36
1975	Mike Schmidt	Philadelphia Phillies	38
1976	Mike Schmidt	Philadelphia Phillies	38
1977	George Foster	Cincinnati Reds	52
1978	George Foster	Cincinnati Reds	40
1979	Dave Kingman	Chicago Cubs	48

NATIONAL LEAGUE [CONTINUED]

YEAR	NAME	TEAM	HRs
1980	Mike Schmidt	Philadelphia Phillies	48
1981	Mike Schmidt	Philadelphia Phillies	31
1982	Dave Kingman	New York Mets	37
1983	Mike Schmidt	Philadelphia Phillies	40
1984	Mike Schmidt	Philadelphia Phillies	36
	Dale Murphy	Atlanta Braves	36
1985	Dale Murphy	Atlanta Braves	37
1986	Mike Schmidt	Philadelphia Phillies	37
1987	Andre Dawson	Chicago Cubs	49
1988	Darryl Strawberry	New York Mets	39
1989	Kevin Mitchell	San Francisco Giants	47
1990	Ryne Sandberg	Chicago Cubs	40
1991	Howard Johnson	New York Mets	38
1992	Fred McGriff	San Diego Padres	35
1993	Barry Bonds	San Francisco Giants	46
1994	Matt Williams	San Francisco Giants	43
1995	Dante Bichette	Colorado Rockies	40
1996	Andres Galarraga	Colorado Rockies	47
1997	Larry Walker	Colorado Rockies	49
1998	Mark McGwire	St. Louis Cardinals	70
1999	Mark McGwire	St. Louis Cardinals	65

140

HOME RUNS BY RIGHT-HANDED BATTERS, LIFETIME

1. Hank Aaron 755
2. Willie Mays 660
3. Frank Robinson 586
4. Harmon Killebrew 573
5. Mike Schmidt 548
6. Jimmie Foxx 534
7. Mark McGwire 522
8. Ernie Banks 512
9. Dave Winfield 465
10. Dave Kingman 442

HOME RUNS BY LEFT-HANDED BATTERS, LIFETIME

1. Babe Ruth 714
2. Reggie Jackson. 563
3. Willie McCovey 521
4. Ted Williams 521
5. Eddie Mathews 512
6. Mel Ott 511
7. Lou Gehrig 493
8. Stan Musial 475
9. Willie Stargell. 475
10. Carl Yastrzemski. 452

HOME RUNS BY SWITCH HITTERS, LIFETIME

1. Mickey Mantle. 536
2. Eddie Murray 504
3. Chili Davis. 350
4. Reggie Smith 314
5. Bobby Bonilla 277
6. Ted Simmons 248
7. Ken Singleton. 246
8. Mickey Tettleton 245
9. Ruben Sierra 239
10. Howard Johnson 228

HOME RUNS IN A SEASON

NAME	TEAM	HRs	YEAR
McGwire, Mark	St. Louis Cardinals	70	1998
Sosa, Sammy	Chicago Cubs	66	1998
McGwire, Mark	St. Louis Cardinals	65	1999
Sosa, Sammy	Chicago Cubs	63	1999
Maris, Roger	New York Yankees	61	1961
Ruth, Babe	New York Yankees	60	1927
Ruth, Babe	New York Yankees	59	1921
Foxx, Jimmie	Philadelphia Athletics	58	1932
Greenberg, Hank	Detroit Tigers	58	1938
McGwire, Mark	Oakland Athletics/ St. Louis Cardinals	58	1997

THE GRAND SLAM

In 1999, bases-loaded home runs flew out of ballparks a total of 139 times (just 2 shy of the '96 record), roundly slamming several marks.

On April 23rd, Fernando Tatis became the first Major Leaguer to hit two grand slams in one inning (the top of the third against the Dodgers). Prior to that inning, the Cardinals third baseman (who batted in 11 runs that day) had precisely 0 career salamis.

Robin Ventura and the grand slam seem to go together.

142

Robin Ventura made his grand entrance into the record book by slamming a bases-clogged round-tripper in each game of a double-header (the only big-leaguer to ever accomplish that feat) against the visiting Milwaukee Brewers on May 20th. The Mets third baseman also became the first player in history to hit two slams in a day twice, having previously whacked four-bags-full four-baggers for the Chicago White Sox against Texas on September 4, 1995.

When Ventura came up with the bases loaded in the first inning of the first game, New York manager Bobby Valentine leaned over to one of his coaches, Bruce Benedict, and said, "It is the year of the grand slam, how about us getting one." Two pitches later, Robin hit one. Ventura's second slam of the day (in the fourth inning of the nightcap) tied him with Mark McGwire and Ken Griffey, Jr. for a career total of 12, only one behind active leader Harold Baines. (On April 30th, Griffey had become the eighteenth Major Leaguer to hit slams in consecutive games.)

Ventura figures in another grand slam scenario. This one occurred in the fifteenth inning of Game 5 of the 1999 National League Championship Series. The Mets and the Braves were tied at 3. Ventura of the home team Mets was up with the bases loaded and nobody out. The outfield was playing in; a long fly ball would bring in the winning run. Ventura left no doubt by smacking a Kevin McGlinchy pitch over the fence for an apparent game-winning grand slam. The score was posted as 7–3. As Ventura attempted to round the bases, he was mobbed by his teammates, eventually taking a shortcut back to the dugout . . . never touching home plate. It was ruled that Ventura's ball, though it cleared the fence, was a single because he never made it past first. Instead of a 7–3 victory and a grand slam, Ventura was credited with a single and the Mets with a 4–3 win.

What's with all of these salamis? Is there a grand plan that can explain them?

"It's a combination of a lot of things," says former Tigers manager Larry Parrish, alluding to livelier, more tightly-wound balls; expansion (diluted, more tightly-wound pitching staffs); smaller stadiums; bigger muscles . . .

But, according to Parrish, perhaps the most significant factor that has put more men on base (and then, in one stroke, removed them) has been "the effort by the umps to tighten up the strike zone. . . . Pretty soon, it gets to a hitter's count, and then the pitcher lays one in, and there she goes."

Don Mattingly, who holds the record for the most grand slams (six) in a season.

MOST GRAND SLAMS, SEASON

6	DON MATTINGLY	NEW YORK YANKEES	1987
5	ERNIE BANKS	CHICAGO CUBS	1955

CAREER LEADERS

LOU GEHRIG	23	BABE RUTH	16
EDDIE MURRAY	19	GIL HODGES	14
WILLIE McCOVEY	18	ROBIN VENTURA	14
JIMMIE FOXX	17	HAROLD BAINES*	13
TED WILLIAMS	17	JOE DiMAGGIO	13
HANK AARON	16	GEORGE FOSTER	13
DAVE KINGMAN	16	RALPH KINER	13

*active

143

HOME RUNS, ONE MONTH

NAME	TEAM	MONTH	HRs
Sammy Sosa	Chicago Cubs	June 1998	20
Rudy York	Detroit Tigers	August 1937	18
Babe Ruth	New York Yankees	September 1927	17
Rudy York	Detroit Tigers	August 1943	17
Willie Mays	San Francisco Giants	August 1965	17
Albert Belle	Cleveland Indians	September 1995	17
Hank Greenberg	Detroit Tigers	September 1946	16
Ralph Kiner	Pittsburgh Pirates	September 1949	16
Mickey Mantle	New York Yankees	May 1956	16
Mark McGwire	St. Louis Cardinals	May 1998	16
Albert Belle	Chicago White Sox	July 1998	16
Mark McGwire	St. Louis Cardinals	July 1999	16

PLAYERS WHO HAVE HIT FOUR HOME RUNS IN A GAME

NAME	TEAM	DATE
Bobby Lowe	Boston Braves	05/30/1894
Ed Delahanty	Philadelphia Phillies	07/13/1896
Lou Gehrig	New York Yankees	06/03/1932
Chuck Klein	Philadelphia Phillies	07/10/1936
Pat Seerey	Chicago White Sox	07/18/1948
Gil Hodges	Brooklyn Dodgers	08/31/1950
Joe Adcock	Milwaukee Braves	07/31/1954
Rocky Colavito	Cleveland Indians	06/10/1959
Willie Mays	San Francisco Giants	04/30/1961
Mike Schmidt	Philadelphia Phillies	04/17/1976
Bob Horner	Atlanta Braves	07/06/1986
Mark Whiten	St. Louis Cardinals	09/07/1993

MOST SEASONS, 50+ HOME RUNS

Mark McGwire	4	Ralph Kiner	2
Babe Ruth	4	Mickey Mantle	2
Jimmie Foxx	2	Willie Mays	2
Ken Griffey, Jr.	2	Sammy Sosa	2

The routes of the four home runs Willie Mays hit in one game against the Milwaukee Braves at Milwaukee County Stadium on April 30, 1961.

MOST CONSECUTIVE SEASONS, 50+ HOME RUNS

Mark McGwire	4	(1996–1999)
Babe Ruth	2	(1920–1921)
Babe Ruth	2	(1927–1928)
Ken Griffey, Jr.	2	(1997–1998)
Sammy Sosa	2	(1998–1999)

MOST SEASONS, 40+ HOME RUNS

Babe Ruth	11	Ernie Banks	5
Hank Aaron	8	Jimmie Foxx	5
Harmon Killebrew	8	Lou Gehrig	5
Ken Griffey, Jr.	6	Juan Gonzalez	5
Willie Mays	6	Ralph Kiner	5
Mark McGwire	6	Duke Snider	5

Most Consecutive Seasons, 40+ Home Runs

Babe Ruth	7	(1926–1932)
Ralph Kiner	5	(1947–1951)
Duke Snider	5	(1953–1957)
Ernie Banks	4	(1957–1960)
Harmon Killebrew	4	(1961–1964)
Ken Griffey, Jr.	4	(1996–1999)
Mark McGwire	4	(1996–1999)
Many tied with	3	

Most Seasons, 30+ Home Runs

Hank Aaron	15	Frank Robinson	11
Babe Ruth	13	Lou Gehrig	10
Mike Schmidt	13	Harmon Killebrew	10
Jimmie Foxx	12	Eddie Mathews	10
Willie Mays	11	Mark McGwire	10

146

Most Consecutive Seasons, 30+ Home Runs

Jimmie Foxx	12	(1929–1940)
Lou Gehrig	9	(1929–1937)
Eddie Mathews	9	(1953–1961)
Mike Schmidt	9	(1979–1987)
Babe Ruth	8	(1926–1933)
Mickey Mantle	8	(1955–1962)
Albert Belle	8	(1992–1999)
Barry Bonds	8	(1992–1999)
Ralph Kiner	7	(1947–1953)
Hank Aaron	7	(1957–1963)
Fred McGriff	7	(1988–1994)

Most Seasons, 20+ Home Runs

Hank Aaron	20	Babe Ruth	16
Willie Mays	17	Ted Williams	16
Frank Robinson	17	Mel Ott	15
Reggie Jackson	16	Willie Stargell	15
Eddie Murray	16	Dave Winfield	15

Ryne Sandberg, who has hit the most home runs in a career for second baseman, poses with Cal Ripken, Jr., who set the same record for shortstop.

MOST CONSECUTIVE SEASONS, 20+ HOME RUNS

Hank Aaron	20	(1955–1974)
Babe Ruth	16	(1919–1934)
Willie Mays	15	(1954–1968)
Eddie Mathews	14	(1952–1965)
Mike Schmidt	14	(1974–1987)
Willie Stargell	13	(1964–1976)
Billy Williams	13	(1961–1973)
Reggie Jackson	13	(1968–1980)
Lou Gehrig	12	(1927–1938)
Jimmie Foxx	12	(1929–1940)
Frank Robinson	12	(1956–1967)
Joe Carter	12	(1986–1997)

MOST GAMES, 3+ HOME RUNS, LIFETIME

Johnny Mize	6	Ralph Kiner	4
Joe Carter	5	Mark McGwire	4
Dave Kingman	5	Larry Parrish	4
Ernie Banks	4	Willie Stargell	4
Lou Gehrig	4	*Many tied with*	3

MOST GAMES, 2+ HOME RUNS, LIFETIME

Babe Ruth	72	Frank Robinson	54
Willie Mays	63	Eddie Mathews	49
Hank Aaron	62	Mel Ott	49
Mark McGwire	62	Harmon Killebrew	46
Jimmie Foxx	55	Mickey Mantle	46

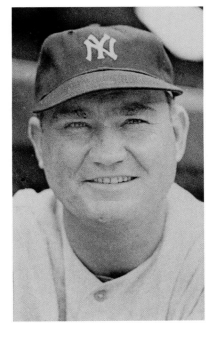

Johnny Mize, who hit three home runs in one game six times in his career.

147

MOST HOME RUNS, LIFETIME, BY POSITION

POSITION	NAME	HRs
1B	Mark McGwire	507
2B	Ryne Sandberg	277
3B	Mike Schmidt	509
SS	Cal Ripken, Jr.	345
OF	Babe Ruth	698
C	Carlton Fisk	351
DH	Harold Baines	224
P	Wes Ferrell	36

MOST HOME RUNS, SINGLE SEASON, BY POSITION

POSITION	NAME	TEAM	YEAR	HRs
1B	Mark McGwire	St. Louis Cardinals	1998	69
2B	Rogers Hornsby	St. Louis Cardinals	1922	42
	Davey Johnson	Atlanta Braves	1973	42
3B	Mike Schmidt	Philadelphia Phillies	1980	48
SS	Ernie Banks	Chicago Cubs	1958	47
OF	Sammy Sosa	Chicago Cubs	1998	66
C	Todd Hundley	New York Mets	1996	41
DH	Rafael Palmeiro	Texas Rangers	1999	37
P	Wes Ferrell	Cleveland Indians	1931	9

Todd Hundley holds the record for most home runs by a catcher in a single season with 41 in 1996.

MOST HOME RUNS, 1900–09

1. Harry Davis 67
2. Piano Legs Hickman 58
3. Sam Crawford 57
4. Buck Freeman 54
5. Socks Seybold 51
6. Honus Wagner 51
7. Nap Lajoie 47
8. Cy Seymour 43
9. Hobe Ferris 40
10. Jimmy Williams 40

MOST HOME RUNS, 1910–19

1. Gavvy Cravath 116
2. Fred Luderus 83
3. Frank Baker 76
4. Wildfire Schulte 75
5. Larry Doyle 64
6. Sherry Magee 61
7. Heinie Zimmerman 58
8. Fred Merkle 57
9. Vic Saier 55
10. Owen Wilson 52

148

Next to Babe Ruth, Rogers Hornsby, seen here, hit more home runs (250) than any other player during the 1920s.

MOST HOME RUNS, 1920–29

1. Babe Ruth 467
2. Rogers Hornsby 250
3. Cy Williams 202
4. Ken Williams 190
5. Jim Bottomley 146
6. Lou Gehrig 146
7. Bob Meusel 146
8. Harry Heilmann 142
9. Hack Wilson 137
10. George Kelly 134

MOST HOME RUNS, 1930–39

1. Jimmie Foxx 415
2. Lou Gehrig 347
3. Mel Ott 308
4. Wally Berger 241
5. Chuck Klein 238
6. Earl Averill 218
7. Hank Greenberg 206
8. Babe Ruth 198
9. Al Simmons 190
10. Bob Johnson 186

149

MOST HOME RUNS, 1940–49

1. Ted Williams 234
2. Johnny Mize 217
3. Bill Nicholson 211
4. Rudy York 189
5. Joe Gordon 181
6. Joe DiMaggio 180
7. Vern Stephens 177
8. Charlie Keller 173
9. Ralph Kiner 168
10. Bobby Doerr 164

MOST HOME RUNS, 1950–59

1. Duke Snider 326
2. Gil Hodges 310
3. Eddie Mathews 299
4. Mickey Mantle 280
5. Stan Musial 266
6. Yogi Berra 256
7. Willie Mays 250
8. Ted Kluszewski 239
9. Gus Zernial 232
10. Ernie Banks 228

150

MOST HOME RUNS, 1960–69

1. Harmon Killebrew 393
2. Hank Aaron 375
3. Willie Mays 350
4. Frank Robinson 316
5. Willie McCovey 300
6. Frank Howard 288
7. Norm Cash 278
8. Ernie Banks 269
9. Mickey Mantle 256
10. Orlando Cepeda 254

Duke Snider hit 326 home runs in the 1950s, more than any other player, including nine members of the elite 500 Club.

MOST HOME RUNS, 1970–79

1. Willie Stargell 296
2. Reggie Jackson 292
3. Johnny Bench 290
4. Bobby Bonds 280
5. Lee May 270
6. Dave Kingman 252
7. Graig Nettles 252
8. Mike Schmidt 235
9. Tony Perez 226
10. Reggie Smith 225

MOST HOME RUNS, 1980–89

1. Mike Schmidt 313
2. Dale Murphy 308
3. Eddie Murray 274
4. Dwight Evans 256
5. Andre Dawson 250
6. Darrell Evans 230
7. Tony Armas 225
8. Lance Parrish 225
9. Dave Winfield 223
10. Jack Clark 216

MOST HOME RUNS, 1990–99

1. Mark McGwire 405
2. Ken Griffey, Jr. 382
3. Barry Bonds 361
4. Albert Belle 351
5. Juan Gonzalez 339
6. Sammy Sosa 332
7. Rafael Palmeiro 328
8. Jose Canseco 303
9. Frank Thomas 301
10. Fred McGriff 300
11. Matt Williams 300

152

Stan "The Man" Musial holds the record for most career All-Star Game home runs with six.

HOME RUNS, ALL-STAR GAME

Stan Musial	6	Rocky Colavito	3
Fred Lynn	4	Harmon Killebrew	3
Ted Williams	4	Ralph Kiner	3
Johnny Bench	3	Willie Mays	3
Gary Carter	3	*14 tied with*	2

HOME RUNS, DIVISION SERIES

Jim Thome	7	Paul O'Neill	6
Ken Caminiti	6	Bernie Williams	6
Juan Gonzalez	6	Nomar Garciaparra	5

HOME RUNS, DIVISION SERIES [CONTINUED]

Ken Griffey, Jr.	5	Jim Leyritz	4
Edgar Martinez	4	Manny Ramirez	4
Chipper Jones	4	John Valentin	4

HOME RUNS, LEAGUE CHAMPIONSHIP SERIES

George Brett	9	Sal Bando	5
Steve Garvey	8	Johnny Bench	5
Darryl Strawberry	7	Ron Gant	5
Reggie Jackson	6	Greg Luzinski	5
Manny Ramirez	6	Gary Matthews, Sr.	5
Jim Thome	6	Graig Nettles	5

Hall of Famer George Brett hit more home runs than any other player (nine) in League Championship Series play.

HOME RUNS, WORLD SERIES

Mickey Mantle	18	Joe DiMaggio	8
Babe Ruth	15	Frank Robinson	8
Yogi Berra	12	Bill Skowron	8
Duke Snider	11	Hank Bauer	7
Lou Gehrig	10	Goose Goslin	7
Reggie Jackson	10	Gil McDougald	7

HOME RUNS, POSTSEASON

Reggie Jackson	18	Yogi Berra	12
Mickey Mantle	18	Steve Garvey	11
Jim Thome	16	Duke Snider	11
Babe Ruth	15	Bernie Williams	11
Manny Ramirez	13	*8 tied with*	10

154

Jim Thome has hit 16 home runs in postseason play, second to Reggie Jackson and Mickey Mantle.

Among Hall of Fame pitcher Robin Roberts's illustrious records is the ignominious honor of allowing the most home runs (505) in a career.

155

HOME RUNS ALLOWED, LIFETIME

1. Robin Roberts 505
2. Ferguson Jenkins 484
3. Phil Niekro 482
4. Don Sutton 472
5. Frank Tanana 448
6. Warren Spahn 434
7. Bert Blyleven 430
8. Steve Carlton 414
9. Gaylord Perry 399
10. Jim Kaat 395

HOME RUNS, ONE "BASEBALL FAMILY"

1. Bonds . . . . 777 (Father Bobby, 332; son Barry, 445)
2. Aaron . . . . 768 (Brothers Hank, 755, and Tommie, 13)
3. DiMaggio . . 573 (Brothers Joe, 361; Vince, 125; and Dom, 87)
4. Griffey . . . . 550 (Father Ken, Sr., 152; son Ken, Jr., 398)
5. Murray . . . . 508 (Brothers Eddie, 504, and Rich, 4)
6. Boyer . . . . . . 444 (Brothers Ken, 282; Clete, 162; and Cloyd, 0)
7. May . . . . 444 (Brothers Lee, 354, and Carlos, 90)
8. Bell . . . . 442 (Grandfather Gus, 206; son Buddy, 201;
   grandson David, 35)
9. Canseco . . . . 431 (Brothers José, 431, and Ozzie, 0)
10. Ripken . . . . 422 (Brothers Cal, 402, and Billy, 20)

156

The father and son duo seen here of father Bobby Bonds (right) and son Barry holds the record for most home runs by a baseball family.

BIBLIOGRAPHY

Creamer, Robert W. *The Babe: The Legend Comes to Life.*
New York: Simon & Schuster, 1974.

Dickson, Paul. *Baseball's Greatest Quotations.* New York:
HarperCollins, 1991.

Gammons, Peter. *Beyond the Sixth Game: What's Happened
to Baseball Since the Greatest Game in World Series History.*
Boston: Houghton Mifflin, 1985.

Honig, Donald. *Baseball America.* New York: Macmillan, 1985.

Koppett, Leonard. *Koppett's Concise History of Major League
Baseball.* Philadelphia: Temple University Press, 1998.

Linn, Ed. *The Great Rivalry: The Yankees and the Red Sox,
1901–1990.* New York: Ticknor & Fields, 1991.

McConnell, Bob, and David Vincent. *SABR Presents: The Home
Run Encyclopedia.* New York: Macmillan, 1996.

Maris, Roger, and Jim Ogle. *Roger Maris at Bat.* New York:
Dual, Sloan & Pierce, 1962.

Ritter, Lawrence S. *Lost Ballparks: A Celebration of Baseball's
Legendary Fields.* New York: Viking Studio Books, 1992.

Robinson, Ray. *The Home Run Heard 'Round the World.*
New York: HarperCollins, 1991.

———. *Baseball Stars of 1961.* New York: Pyramid, 1961.

———. *Ted Williams.* New York: Putnam, 1962.

———. *Iron Horse: Lou Gehrig in His Time.* New York:
W.W. Norton, 1990.

Robinson, Ray, and Christopher Jennison. *Yankee Stadium:
75 Years of Drama, Glamor, and Glory.* New York:
Penguin Studio Books, 1998.

Schreiber, Lee R. *Race for the Record: The Great Home Run Chase
of 1998.* New York: HarperCollins, 1998.

Silverman, Al. *The World of Sport*. New York: Holt, Rinehart, & Winston, 1962.

———. *The Best of Sport: 1946–1971*. New York: Viking Books, 1971.

Silverman, Al, and Brian Silverman. *The Twentieth Century Treasury of Sports*. New York: Viking Books, 1992.

Tackach, James. *Baseball Legends—Hank Aaron*. Philadelphia: Chelsea House Publishers, 1992.

Thorn, John, and Michael Gershman. *Total Baseball: The Ultimate Encyclopedia of Baseball*. New York: 1989.

Wimmer, Dick. *The Home Run Game*. Short Hills, N.J.: Burford Books, 1999.

INDEX

161

PHOTO CREDITS

166

Page 104 AP/Wide World Photos (Bump Wills)
and AP/Wide World Photos
(Toby Harrah)

Page 105 National Baseball Library/MLB
Photos (Jesse Burkett) and AP/Wide
World Photos (Willie Wilson)

HOME RUN DERBY

Page 106 National Baseball Library/MLB
Photos

Page 108 AP/Wide World Photos

Page 109 National Baseball Library/MLB
Photos

Page 111 AP/Wide World Photos

Page 112 AP/Wide World Photos (M&M Boys)

Pages 112-113 AP/Wide World Photos
(Roger Maris)

Page 114 AP/Wide World Photos

Page 115 AP/Wide World Photos

Page 116 AP/Wide World Photos

Page 117 AP/Wide World Photos

Page 118 AP/Wide World Photos

Page 119 AP/Wide World Photos

Page 120 AP/Wide World Photos

Page 121 AP/Wide World Photos

Page 122 AP/Wide World Photos

Page 123 AP/Wide World Photos

Page 124 Ron Vesely/MLB Photos

Page 125 AP/Wide World Photos

Page 126 AP/Wide World Photos

Page 127 Ronald Hickman/MLB Photos

Page 128 National Baseball Library/MLB
Photos

Page 129 AP/Wide World Photos

Page 131 Photofile/MLB Photos (Rocky
Colavito) and National Baseball
Library/MLB Photos (Dick Stuart)

HOME RUN STATISTICS

Page 132 National Baseball Library/MLB
Photos

Page 136 Rich Pilling/MLB Photos

Page 138 AP/Wide World Photos

Page 142 Bob Rosato/MLB Photos

Page 143 Rich Pilling/MLB Photos

Page 145 AP/Wide World Photos

Page 146 Rich Pilling/MLB Photos

Page 147 Photofile/MLB Photos

Page 148 Rich Pilling/MLB Photos

Page 149 National Baseball Library/MLB
Photos

Page 151 Photofile/MLB Photos

Page 152 Photofile/MLB Photos

Page 153 Dan Donovan/MLB Photos

Page 154 Photfile/MLB Photos

Page 155 Photofile/MLB Photos

Page 156 AP/Wide World Photos

167

ABOUT THE AUTHORS

ROBERT W. CREAMER was a member of the original staff of *Sports Illustrated* and has written for the magazine for nearly half a century. His biography of Babe Ruth, *Babe: The Legend Comes to Life,* has been in print for twenty-five years. His other books include the biography *Stengel: His Life and Times* and the memoir *Baseball and Other Matters in 1941.*

ELIAS SPORTS BUREAU compiled the statistics for this book. It is the official statistician of Major League Baseball, the National Football League, and the National Basketball Association.

DAVID HALBERSTAM, journalist and historian, is a Pulitzer Prize winner (1964) for his reporting from Vietnam for the *New York Times.* Late in his career as a political writer he returned to writing about sports; he has written five books on the subject, all of which have been bestsellers. He is also the editor of *The Best American Sports Writing of the Century.*

DONALD HONIG has published more than seventy-five books, including sixteen novels and forty on the subject of baseball. Some of those about baseball include *Baseball When the Grass Was Real, October Heroes,* and *Baseball America.*

LEONARD KOPPETT has been covering baseball since 1949 for major papers in New York and California and is the only writer named to the writers' wing of both the baseball and basketball Halls of Fame. His two latest books are *Koppett's Concise History of Major League Baseball,* and *The Man in the Dugout.*

ED LINN was considered one of the notable writers on sports in the twentieth century. He was a contributing editor to *Sport* magazine and authored seventeen books, including three with maverick baseball owner Bill Veeck, the most famous of those being *Veeck—As in Wreck*. He also collaborated with Sandy Koufax and Leo Durocher on their autobiographies, *Koufax* and *Nice Guys Finish Last*, and is the author of the critically acclaimed *Hitter: The Life and Turmoils of Ted Williams*.

RAY ROBINSON is the former magazine editor of *Pageant, Coronet, Good Housekeeping, Seventeen,* and *TV Guide*. He is also the author of innumerable books, including *Yankee Stadium: 75 Years of Drama, Glamour, and Glory; The Home Run Heard 'Round the World; Iron Horse: Lou Gehrig in His Time; Matty: An American Hero;* and *Rockne of Notre Dame: The Making of a Football Legend*. He lives in New York City with his wife, Phyllis, and his Norwich terrier, Penelope.

LEE R. SCHREIBER is a New York–based writer and editor who has contributed to *GQ*, the *New York Times Magazine*, and *TV Guide*, among numerous other publications. The author of eight books, including *Race for the Record* (HarperCollins)—the definitive account of 1998's great home run chase—he's currently editor-at-large of *Pro*, a new magazine for professional athletes.

BRIAN SILVERMAN, a writer and editor, was the coeditor of the highly acclaimed sports anthology, *The Twentieth Century Treasury of Sports*. He is the author of two novels and several books on sports. He lives in New York with his wife, Heather, and son, Louis.

BERRY STAINBACK, the former editor of *Sport* magazine and coauthor of the bestseller *Snake*, the autobiography of Ken Stabler, has also cowritten autobiographies of baseball legends Frank Robinson and Earl Weaver.

BOBBY THOMSON was a three-time National League All-Star, batted in 100 runs or more in four different seasons, and hit 264 home runs in a 15-year major league career. He is best known, however, for "the shot heard 'round the world," his three-run home run to win the National League pennant for the New York Giants on October 3, 1951.